THE BEGINNER'S GUIDE TO
LIVING OFF-THE-GRID

THE DIY WORKBOOK FOR LIVING THE LIFE YOU WANT

GARY COLLINS, MS

The Beginner's Guide to Living Off the Grid
By Gary Collins

ISBN: 978-0-941678-11-7

Printed and bound in the United States of America.

Publisher: Bill Uhler
Editorial Director: Oscar H. Will III
Merchandise and Event Director: Andrew Perkins
Production Director: Bob Cucciniello
Special Content Editorial Director: Christian Williams
Special Content Group Editor: Jean Teller
Special Content Assistant Editor: Haleigh McGavoock
Book Design and Layout: Amanda Barnwell

All photos courtesy Getty Images, Adobe Stock,
and the author unless otherwise noted

1503 S.W. 42nd St.
Topeka, KS 66609, USA
Telephone (785) 274-4300
Fax (785) 274-4305
www.ogdenpubs.com

Author's Note

Get Your Free Goodies and
Be a Part of My Special Community!

Building a solid relationship with my readers is incredibly important to me. It's one of the rewards of being a writer. From time to time, I send out my newsletter (never spammy, I promise) to keep you up-to-date with special offers and information about anything new I may be doing. I have moved away from using social media in the pursuit of a simpler life, so if you want to be part of the "in crowd," my newsletter and blog are the place to be.

If that's not enough enticement, when you sign up for my newsletter, I'll send you some spectacular free stuff:

• 10% off with free shipping for your first order on my website, www.thesimplelifenow.com
• The complete list of my solar system products and components
• My list of essential living off-the-grid products and resources
• Chapter 4 on how to deal with contractors from Gary's book Living Off The Grid

You can get all the goodies above by signing up for my mailing list at www.thesimplelifenow.com/offgridworkbook

Other Books by Gary Collins

Introduction:
What is this Book About?

My first two books on the subject of off-the-grid living: *Going Off The Grid* and the follow up *Living Off The Grid* are more focused on how I found my property, built my house off the grid, and the lessons learned along the way. Not to say, these two books are not filled with a great deal of how-to and do-it-yourself information, but I felt in order for you to map out your plan of living off the grid or a more remote lifestyle a workbook would be of a huge benefit.

As I have said, when I started on my journey over a decade ago, there was not a lot of information on how to get started living this type of lifestyle. Basically, I had to figure out a lot of it on my own, which took a lot more time and financial resources. I have also said on numerous occasions, this is your journey so trying to do it just like me is not really doable in most cases, as your wants and needs will be different. With that being said, I do believe giving people a process to develop a plan in order to pursue this type of life will make the journey far easier. From the responses I have received over the years, people have indicated the information on my blog (www.thesimplelifenow.com) and in my books has helped them to save time, money, and, most importantly, what to expect while pursuing and living this lifestyle.

While writing my book *Living Off The Grid*, I thought, "Wouldn't it be great to have a book where people can organize and put their plan together?"

Any of you who follow me and read my books know I'm a big stickler for having a plan. Going about things willy-nilly or flying by the seat of your pants in anything is just a bad idea, especially when you're considering a huge life change. Not to say that at times you will have to deviate from your original plan, but if you have an organized and systematic game plan while pursuing this life it will be much, much easier. I have lost count over the years the people I have met who were full of fire to get started buying their land and building a house off-the-grid, to flame out in less than a year. All had a common theme ... no real plan, just went about it on a whim.

You may be asking why not write a comprehensive book outlining all the things about my project, how to do it, and a planning workbook. One important thing I have learned by being an avid reader and educator: Too much information in one place is a bad thing. First, the other topics will suffer as you are trying to

stuff 10 pounds of crap in a 5-pound bag. Secondly, people learn much better when given information in smaller chunks (me included). All the best how-to books I have read during my life are short usually less than 150 pages. My goal is to make sure you can take the information I provide and put it into practice … quickly and efficiently in bite size chunks. I believe this workbook will be indispensable for those ready to put their plan together for living a simpler and happier life. I know I wish I had these types of books when I first started, as it would have made my process much easier. That is where my off-the-grid series comes from; to help those interested in pursuing the life they want to live.

This book will not only give you some valuable information, but a place to put together lists that are essential to your overall plan. It is meant to be a book you can carry around and fill in as you go, this way you have all that handy-dandy information in one spot! I do not say this just to sell more books, but I think it would probably be a good idea to get a couple copies of this book, so you can transfer over old information and make updated changes as your plan moves along. There is nothing worse than trying to read through scribble outs and notes from different time periods. One thing I can guarantee is your plan is going change and evolve as you move along in the process.

I will leave you with this—spending five years building my house with learning a lot of lessons along the way was one of the hardest things I have ever done, but I don't regret it for a second. My life is so different from the average American's today (in a good way), far less stressful, living life on my own terms, and just flat out being happier and more content with my life in general.

As with all my books I hope this one helps you reach your dreams and aspirations of living a simpler and happier life.

CHAPTER 1

My Story: How My Mobile Lifestyle Began

In the next couple chapters, I will cover how I started on my journey of living off the grid. I have included this information in some of my previous books, so you can skip ahead to chapter 3 if you have previously read it. If you are still on the fence though, it might be a good review to light a fire under your butt to get going!

If this is the first book of mine you have read, I would highly recommend you read the next couple chapters, as it is my story, and I believe there are some valuable life lessons that I learned.

Dealing with Today's Life Grind

As most of you who follow me or have read my book *Going Off The Grid* know, my journey didn't start on a whim. I constructed the foundation of how I live over a decade ago. It started as a desire to live more remotely and simply, then it evolved into a complete lifestyle change.

First, I think it is important to understand that I grew up in a small town in the mountains of California, so living off the grid in the Pacific Northwest is not as drastic a stretch for me as one might think. I did not go into this adventure completely in the dark.

During my life, I have lived in many cities across the country. As I have aged, I have become more disenchanted with and disengaged from that type of living. Urban living is not a bad lifestyle; it's just not for me anymore.

Having grown up poor in a single-wide trailer, with very few neighbors, you would think I would not ever want to return to such a lifestyle. That couldn't be further from the truth. Having grown up that way has given me a different perspective on what I truly think is important. Sure, at times things were tough growing up, but it made me appreciate everything I had that much more. I now look back and consider myself incredibly lucky to have had these experiences. I was fortunate enough to know most of the people in my town. I was able to wave at them and get a wave back in return. That is pretty much unheard of in an urban setting today.

I still have fond memories of racing home from football practice before the sun went down to get in an hour of bird hunting. Heck, I would have my shotgun behind the seat of my truck to save time. Yes, that would mean I had a shotgun on school grounds, and I wouldn't have been the only one. A lot of us were hunters, and that was just all there was to it. Can you imagine what would happen to a kid doing that today?

Once I left for college at eighteen, I had very few opportunities to do the things I enjoyed doing while growing up— hiking, fishing, hunting … just being in nature. For many years I had yearned to return to that type of living. It is hard to explain to someone who has never experienced this lifestyle, but for me, spending time outdoors always made me the happiest.

To me, the daily grind of living in congested areas has become completely overwhelming and too stressful. Why would I want to sit in traffic if I don't have to? The thought of going to the mall actually makes me cringe to say the least.

Now I can't state this enough: there was a lot of planning with numerous false starts and mistakes made along the way. With that being said, I wouldn't change a thing. Well, maybe I wish someone had already written the books I have put together, as it would have made my life much easier.

Like most people today, I was doing the day-to-day grind and had spent almost half my life working for the government in one form or another. Needless to say, I was completely burned out and was questioning numerous aspects of my life. I remember just sitting there at my desk, after another joyous meeting with one of my bosses, thinking, "What the heck am I doing with my life?" Now, I knew I needed a plan, but what was that plan? I had a house that was ridiculously expensive, with more debt than I wanted or was really necessary, and I was living in congested Southern California slowly losing my mind.

I know now that the dissatisfaction with my previous lifestyle and mindset is not an unusual sentiment. I remember thinking, "Is there something wrong with me?"

I have spoken to and received emails from hundreds and hundreds of people who feel exactly as I do. If you feel this way, you are not alone. Today there a lot more groups who are looking for or actually living the same type of lifestyle I live today. Simply put, we are not willing to accept the modern-day societal expectation that we grind ourselves to oblivion chasing someone else's predefined idea of happiness ... there has to be a better way!

The Search Begins ... Kind Of

The original plan just simply started; I wanted to find someplace quiet to get away. So I started looking at remote land or cabins in Oregon, Washington, Wyoming, and Montana. It was just a cursory look. As it was in the middle of the housing boom, I soon noticed that remote properties were just as overpriced as the typical family dwelling in more populated areas. I called a couple realtors just to get some information, but nothing serious came of it. At this point I was a little discouraged that my plan was nothing more than a dream.

I shelved my plan and continued with my daily grind, discouraged. What I have found, after over a decade of research, is that everyone goes through this type of discouragement.

Another important point I need to make is I have never fit into the mold of today's American lifestyle: the nine-to-five jobs, the commute, the cookie-cutter suburban homes. I started my own side business a good ten years prior to hatching my idea of a mobile lifestyle in an effort to break out. I have always been more of a "free thinker." I knew that in order to really have freedom, I would have to run not only my own life, but possibly my own business. Let me assure you, though, while I don't think it is 100 percent necessary for you to run your own business to live a more mobile lifestyle, it sure helps. The best advice I can give is if you are feeling the grind and are really serious about living a simpler or more mobile lifestyle, you need to come up with a business model that fits this type of lifestyle. Today, telecommuting is becoming more common for certain jobs that do not require you to be in an office day to day, so just because you have a nine-to-five job doesn't mean you can't live this type of lifestyle.

A Kick in the Butt—The Real Search Begins

Fast-forward to 2013, and all these thoughts were still in the back of my mind. But due to many life-changing circumstances, I wasn't really pursing my dream; I was in a rut. In that year, the stress of trying to run my own business weighed on me and numerous recent deaths of loved ones,

including one of my best friends, hit home. I knew if I kept saying, "I will get to it next year," it would never happen.

So with that, I rekindled the dream and put a plan into action. From the time when I had originally thought about living a simpler, more remote lifestyle, my ideas had evolved and changed. I had started a new business, sold my house and most of my belongings, and was debt free. I was in a much better place to really pursue my dream. My original plan was to have a remote getaway; now it was to live off the grid for at least part of the year, dedicating myself to being more mobile rather than stuck in one place. I was fortunate while working in the government to have traveled all over the world, but this lifestyle is addictive. I had caught the nomadic bug—I realized I just couldn't stay in one place for very long. In addition, the housing bubble had taught me that the supposed American dream of home ownership—with that big fat mortgage—is a chain around the ankle of a freedom-based lifestyle.

Most think that living a mobile lifestyle or living off the grid means living in a beat-up van, cave, or shack with no running water or electricity. Today that couldn't be further from the truth. You can now live a comfortable life on a piece of fairly isolated land or travel around in a state-of-the-art RV. I know this for a fact! Not only have I been doing it for years now, but I have run into more people than I can count who are doing the same thing or something very similar.

OK, I am going to address this now, as it is the main argument I get from people who think what I do is not obtainable for most people because I'm single with no children. I could go into a long diatribe about life decisions and lifestyle choices, but I will not—maybe in another book. (Haha, just kidding.) The fact is I have met so many people who are married with two to three children, not to mention multiple pets, who are living exactly like I am. I'm telling you with firsthand knowledge: Anyone can live this lifestyle successfully if they want to. It all boils down to whether you want it and make it happen proactively or whether you just want to make excuses and complain about your life. Yes, it's a little tough love, but someone has to say it. This life is as simple as coming up with a plan and putting it into action, instead of waiting for a miracle to happen, which will more than likely never occur.

I think the best part of this adventure is I'm funding it in a way that most Americans can afford. I do not come from a long line of millionaires, and I do not have unlimited resources. Still, I won't deny, it does cost money, especially in the beginning. I know there are shows and books that say you can just take off with a hundred bucks in your pocket and do it. And some people have done it that way, but I like to live in reality and talk about what is plausible for most people, not a selective few.

Hopefully you will enjoy my adventure, and even if you are not interested in such a lifestyle, maybe you will learn a little something that you can incorporate into your life to make it simpler and more enjoyable.

CHAPTER 2

So Where Do You Start?
You Have Too Much Crap!

When you are thinking about living a more mobile lifestyle or even contemplating simplifying your life, I think you need a solid starting point. As I preach in my other books—it is always better to have a plan and to take it slow in the beginning. Many people, caught up in our society's instant-gratification thought process, forget that great things come with time and perseverance.

As you now know, my off-the-grid life and journey of simplification started several years ago when I decided to downsize. After owning several homes that were much bigger than I needed and filled with crap that I would never use, I decided it was time for a change.

The bottom line is, if you are truly interested in this type of lifestyle, you are going to have to downsize ... and for most of you, you'll have to downsize big time! Don't be one of those people with a convoy of moving trucks moving all your crap from the city to the country. If you haven't figured out my philosophy of living off the grid, it is not to just re-locate, but to live a simpler life. You can't do that with a ton of junk weighing you down.

Consumer Nation: Buying Everything in Sight Doesn't Equal Happiness

Just like most people today, I had spent my life being just what society and the system wanted me to be: the ultimate consumer. It is no secret that our lives suffer under maximum workloads in order to make money so that we can buy as much as we can to fill the unhappiness void. Now, I'm not saying there is no value in work, and I don't begrudge working hard and earning an honest wage, but I do think we have our priorities way out of whack today.

Why do we purchase the biggest house we can obtain and shackle ourselves to its suffocating loan? Why do we buy that sports car we really can't afford? Why do we have a closet full of clothes and shoes we hardly wear? In the end, we stress ourselves out so we can obtain all these items, and for what? Exactly! You can't answer that question because there is no logical or reasonable answer.

To me, the answer is simple. We do all the above, and drive ourselves crazy in the process, because that is what we have been told to do in order to find happiness. So, in today's society, stuff equals happiness. Trust me, I followed this mantra with gusto, purchasing all kinds of junk I didn't need.

Stop Being a Crap Collector

So where do you start? Well just like any addict, admit you have a problem. I like to attribute the moniker "junkaholic" to the affliction most of us suffer from today. As a human, it might seem like your primary goal in life is to compile as much useless stuff as you can, and then die among the heaps of your ingloriously obtained items in the hopes that someone finds you before one of your pets starts eating your face. OK, I know that is a little over the top, but I think you see my point.

Just as I said above, the starting point is realizing that your life means more than your stuff. It would be further fulfilled by creating experiences rather than by acquiring shiny items. The luster of objects lasts for a very short time, then you need another shiny object to fill its void. Remember not too long ago us hairless apes could carry all of our belongings on our backs!

For me, I just had to realize that less was more. Just like my optimal health philosophy, the interpretation of less will be different for each individual: having a more mobile life will mean keeping your house but having a getaway or selling your house and renting, going on occasional adventures in an RV, or going all in living off the grid or traveling in an RV full-time. As for me, I wanted to live in a comfortable, up-to-date home off the grid but also spend part of the year going on adventures towing a travel trailer. In other words, less junk, fewer headaches, and more time for what truly matters in life ... while still living in the modern world part time. I knew I wouldn't be able to do this if I held onto a bunch of useless crap; I had to make a choice.

The starting point for me was to greatly downsize my living space. Back then, I was paying a ridiculous mortgage for a 1,700-square-foot house in Southern California and losing sleep constantly trying to figure out how to pay for it. I was single and had two dogs. Why I thought I needed this much space, even today, is a mystery to me. Well, not really. I had been brainwashed into thinking bigger was better. In the end, all it did was stress me out, financially and emotionally, and make me spend a great deal of time on upkeep when I could have been using that time doing something I truly enjoyed. That is one important point I want to make about our modern maximum-consumption lifestyle: Instead of making us happy, in the end it actually makes us less happy and takes time away from our true passions and those individuals we care about. If that isn't true irony, I don't know what is.

We spend a great deal of our lives pursuing the things that we have been told will make us happy, but in the end, they make us miserable and unfulfilled. Wow, the joke is on us. The great news is that we can change this, and I want to share with you my experience, and the steps you can take in order to happify (my made-up word) and simplify!

Evaluate Your Current Living Conditions

The first thing you need to analyze is your current living situation. Can you get by with less living space? I would say almost everyone in this country could answer this with a resounding yes! If you live in a standard-size American house, and you say no, I'm pretty sure this off grid or mobile lifestyle is not for you. But at the same time, that doesn't mean you can't take this information and downsize to a more affordable, smaller house. I know this book is primarily about mobile and off grid living, but I'm a big believer in life simplification in general.

For those who are interested in life simplification, make sure to check out my *The Simple Life* book series.

The first thing I did was simple—I analyzed my monthly cost-of-living expenses. This included my mortgage, insurance, utilities, and general upkeep expenses. It came out to an astounding $3,500 a month.

For those of you who do not live in California, or one of the more expensive states, you are probably flabbergasted by that amount. Let me tell you, that is cheap in Southern California. Most people I know in California easily spend around $5,000 to $6,000 or more, for what I outlined above. Now that I look back with my "what is important to me" clarity, this was absolutely nuts.

19

For me, I still had about twenty-seven years left on my mortgage, so that meant I could look forward to spending a total of $1,134,000 (yes, that is over a million dollars) if I maintained that type of lifestyle for the remainder of my mortgage. Here is the kicker: Most of us don't maintain; we upgrade. So for most of us, that total would actually go up.

Basically, we all have the capability of being millionaires if we just adjusted our lifestyles choices. That is a pretty astounding statement. Just thinking of the average person I know in California, their total would be close to double mine, if not more. I hope you are starting to see the insanity of our consumer-based economy in this country.

Most of you might think my example is rather dramatic, but I assure you, once I got settled in my new, downsized place, it was anything but. As I outlined, I was living in the typical Southern California residential neighborhood in a home with three bedrooms, two bathrooms, and a two-car garage. For a single guy, this is just way too much space. Heck, I think it is too big for the average family, and I will explain why later.

Is Renting an Option?

The reason I bring up renting as an option is because it is a good transition if you are a homeowner who is planning to sell. Renting gives you a go-between while you downsize and get your plan together, but it avoids the need to make a big leap. It's getting your toes wet, wading into a simpler life in a smaller dwelling. Obviously, you don't want to rent a place the same size or bigger than what you have already; you have to downsize, which will force you to get rid of the dogs-playing-poker print on the wall in that dusty man cave.

That being said, I do know people who skipped this step, sold the house and all their stuff and never looked back. Again this all comes down to your goals and lifestyle plans.

After analyzing how much my house cost each month, I decided to take a look at renting and see what made sense. I realized I needed time to get my finances in order, work further on my business, and finalize my plan to simplify my life. The first place I checked out was on Craigslist.com.

I will tell you, it was very discouraging in the beginning; renting in California is fairly expensive when compared with the rest of the country. As I write this, another housing boom is overtaking California, and the prices are even higher than the previous one. I guess some of us never learn from the past.

Not to mention, back when I was looking to rent, it was just after the housing bubble had burst (the start of the Great Recession), so everyone was trying to do what I was doing. The glut of prospective renters was pushing rents even higher. The icing on the cake was having two large dogs; most rental owners really don't like pets, and if they do accept them, they almost always hit you with a significant up-charge.

So what did that mean? Instead of renting in my general location, I had to cast a wider net in order to find more options. Having pets meant I had to look in more rural areas where people didn't really care as much about renting to people who have pets. I started by looking for two-bedroom places, and quickly realized the price difference between what I was currently paying and the prospective rental was not large enough to justify this choice.

This forced me to start looking outside my perceived comfort zone. I began investigating studios, granny flats (small apartments attached to houses), and cottages (basically a studio house in which all living space is concentrated in one area as with a studio apartment).

This search opened an entirely new lifestyle that I had never experienced before; it simplified living far more than what I was used to. It is amazing: having less space forces you to have less stuff, which ultimately makes you happier. I'll be honest I really didn't see that happening in the beginning of my search.

Sometimes you might get lucky and find the place you want right away, but from my experience, making such a drastic change takes time. Here is why:

• *Unless you have lived this way before, these could be neighborhoods or dwellings you have never experienced before.*
• *You will probably have to search in new areas that you are unfamiliar with, and determine which works best for your current situation.*

Here is the key: Change is always painful in the beginning, and there is no getting around this. You have to realize you are making a major life change, and it is going to be uncomfortable. All great things in life come with some scrapes and bruises along the way.

My search for a rental home in Southern California took several months—six to be exact. I did a lot of research and soul-searching during this period, and ultimately, it paid off. I found a cottage with a full-size yard located in a rural part of San Diego.

In the end, by being patient, it ended up being the nicest place I had found, and it had the lowest rent, to the tune of several hundred dollars! Ironically, my landlords were the best I have ever had. When you take your time and are patient, a little luck will come your way.

I will emphasize that when renting you need to really evaluate your landlords just like they are evaluating you. For most, moving is not a pleasant experience, so my philosophy is why do it more than you have to! When I moved into my new-to-me rental in San Diego, I knew I would be there for at least two years. I ended up being there over four years.

That is another key thing to think about. How long do you plan to live in this place? Can you stay longer, if need be? If you own, will you be able to sell your house in a timely manner, or will you have to try and turn your former home into a rental?

In my situation, I was unsure how long I would be there, but I made sure it was something I could do long term if I needed to. Thankfully, I had thought that through because I ended up being in the cottage rental far longer than I had originally expected.

I know most of you who are married and have children are going, "Yeah, that is no problem for a single guy, but our situation is different." Yes and no. I know families who have reduced their living area by half with no problem at all. Sure, at first, they and their children had to get used to the new lifestyle, but once they adapted, I never heard one complaint about not having enough space. Again, it is about facing the challenge and not giving in to the sentiment that "it is just too hard."

Simplifying your life comes with challenges, and you have to keep your eye on the prize at the end. More financial stability and less stuff ultimately means more freedom. I'm not saying that minimizing your living space and having more disposable income is the solution to all your life problems. But I can promise you this: It is easier to figure them out without additional, self-perpetuated stress.

The Pay Off

The Recession was not kind to most of us. I'll be honest, I ended up selling my house for a significant loss, but I had to make a critical choice. Let the house eventually push me into bankruptcy or sacrifice short-term loss for long-term happiness. These were incredibly tough circumstances, but I don't regret what I did for a second. I want to emphasize this is the decision I made, but I'm not a financial expert. You will have to weigh your own circumstances and determine what is best for you and your family.

The payoff for me was undeniable. By forcing myself way out of my comfort zone, I found a great rental place for a great price. Now, I know you are asking, "So how big was the cottage?" My new rental place was around 475 square feet (based on my measurements). That's right, I went from 1,700 to 475 square feet, almost a 75 percent reduction in living space!

Do I recommend everyone make such a drastic change? Of course not. Again, it depends on your situation and your comfort levels. I will tell you that I have no regrets and the thought of ever living in a big house again has not once crossed my mind since I made the change.

Now let's get down to the nitty-gritty—so how much did I save? I was able to go down from $3,500 in basic living expenses per month to $1,100 a month. The best part for me was not just saving a lot of money but also not having all the stress of maintaining and paying for a large house. That was priceless.

Another bonus was that I had to sell a lot of stuff because there was no way it was going to fit into the rental cottage. I made close to $10,000 selling all my extra crap on Craigslist, and I sold most of it in forty-eight hours! I can't explain the cleansing effect this had on my psyche and life. After selling all those useless possessions, it felt as if a huge weight had been lifted off my shoulders. I draw the above advice from my real-life experience. As most of you know from my other books, I never give you advice about things I have never done myself.

I have learned that home ownership not only costs you financially, but it can also put you in a situation where you can get stuck. I used my time in the rental place to plot out my next move (which turned out to be my mobile lifestyle and off-the-grid project!) and make sure I was not rushing into anything I would later regret. I know not everything can be planned for, nor does everything always work out perfectly, but I like to give myself the best odds possible to avoid as many pitfalls as I can.

Operation Travel Trailer: Hello Tiny Living

As I explained above, this renting period taught me how to downsize; it also bought me time to get my ultimate plan together. By the time I had been renting for about three years, I had purchased my twenty acres for my off-the-grid house project. I was ready for the next step.

I found that while building a house off the grid, a great way to enjoy the property and save money is to live in an RV on the property. Matter of fact, I have learned that this is how most people build an off-the-grid house. For most, because there is no financing for off-the-grid homes, it usually takes three to five years to complete the project. The upside is you usually have no or very little debt when it is done; the downside is you need someplace to live for the duration. For those interested in the off-the-grid lifestyle, I highly recommend you get my book *Going Off The Grid*, as it is a step-by-step how-to-book. For me, I planned to live the mobile and off-the-grid lifestyle, so I now needed to get a travel trailer.

Whoops, A Snag In Operation Travel Trailer

As I said in the beginning, I share it all, good and bad. I thought I had the perfect strategy living on my property in my travel trailer, until I built my house. This is where my inexperience with travel trailers bit me in the butt. At this time I had a 4x4 V6 Toyota Tacoma, and my travel trailer was an 18-foot Ultra Lite, which is made to be towed by smaller vehicles. There were a few problems with my plan:

• My property had terrible roads
• The roads are very steep
• My truck didn't have anywhere near the power to tow a trailer in these conditions
• If I was able to get the travel trailer to the property there was no way I was getting it out

Luckily, I decided to do some recon before I towed my trailer up, and realized my original plan wasn't going to work. Did I panic? Well, maybe a little, but what it did do was make me look around for RV parks, and I found were more than enough in the area, and they ended up costing me about $300 a month. I stayed at two different RV parks while building my house, and, to be honest, it wasn't bad and in the end made running my business while building the house a lot easier.

For those interested in more information on RV living, I cover this material in my book, *The Simple Life Guide To RV Living: The Road to Freedom and Mobile Lifestyle Revolution*.

CHAPTER 3

How To Get Started
With Your Plan and Goals

From here on out you will be filling out step-by-step information for your plan, as I have provided the space for numerous lists and a place for notes at the end of this book. I have put together what I consider to be a logical order to follow while pursuing the purchasing and building of your off-grid or remote property. This is not put into stone; feel free to jump around as your plan comes together, but I would recommend you follow this order as best you possibly you can. Again, probably not a bad idea to have a couple of these workbooks to use, as your plan moves along.

Coming Up With Your Initial Plan

The old saying comes to mind, "You have to learn to crawl before you walk," when starting on the path to living off the grid. I constantly get people asking me about living off the grid and how to get started; when I respond, "do you have an initial plan," I'm usually met with a blank stare. So what would an initial or starting plan look like you might ask?

When I consult with people about getting started, the first thing I ask is, "What is your current living situation?" The reason I ask this is that this will determine the first stages

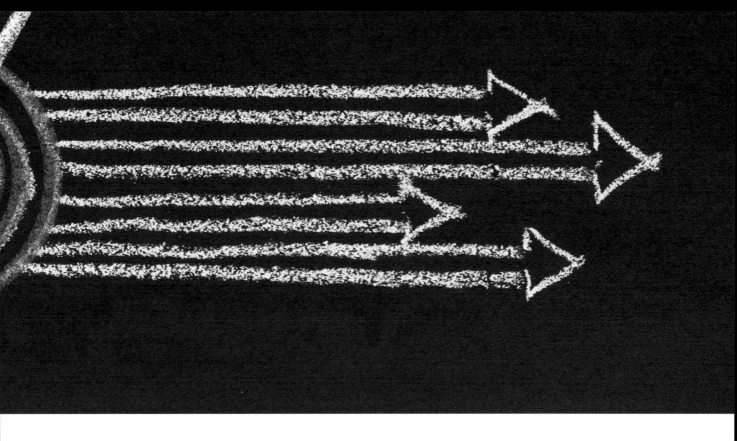

of your plan. Why would I not ask first about your wants and needs in this type of lifestyle? Simply, you will probably need to adjust your current living situation in order to take the first step in your adventure. Most Americans' current living situation is far different than living off the grid. As you saw, I go over this a bit in my own situation in the previous chapter.

The list of questions I start with are:

- Do you own your home?
- Do you rent?
- Do you have a mortgage?
- How much is your monthly house payment?
- Are you in a market where you can sell your house easily?
- How fast are you looking to get started?
- How much savings do you have?
- How much debt do you have?
- How will you sustain yourself financially while living off the grid?

The first question you need to ask yourself, if you own your home, is are you willing to sell it, or do you want to try and rent it out? I cannot do this for you, as you will need to determine the good and bad points of selling or renting your current residence. I will say for most, you will not be living in the same area as your current house, probably not even in the same state when going off the grid, so dealing with

a long distance rental could turn into a stressful situation. Also, some Americans owe more than their house is worth, so are you willing to take a loss to pursue your off-the-grid dream?

As you are starting to see, this first step is critical. For me, it took me about six months to a year to figure out how to deal with my house and move to the next step of my plan.

If you are a renter, you are in a good position, but, until you make the next step, you need to determine if it is time and cost effective to move to a smaller rental in order to save additional money. Even possibly moving into a RV, which is what I did to save even more money.

This is a good time to mention this as we tend to get way ahead of ourselves in our instant gratification society today. On average, to include my own off-the-grid project and talking with numerous others, it takes about three to five years for people to make the transition from living their current lifestyle to finishing their off-the-grid house. So be patient, don't rush the process, just keep plugging along.

Determining Your Finances

When pursing this type of lifestyle, there will be two critical factors that will determine your chances of success:

1. A good plan
2. Finances

Again I have met a ton of people who jump into this lifestyle without any type of financial resources, not only to start their off-the-grid project, but to sustain their lifestyle long-term.

I have found two major sticking points when people want to change their life for the better:

1. Changing their health
2. Getting their finances in order

For a total health reboot check out my book, *The Simple Life Guide To Optimal Health,* and be on the lookout for my next book in *The Simple Life* series: *The Simple Life Guide To Decluttering Your Life*, as I will address both of these issues in great detail.

The first thing I need you to do after evaluating your current living situation, and the action you need to take from there, is do a financial analysis of your total debt. I don't know why this is, but people absolutely hate doing this step, and skip it more often than not. I will say this with emphasis (think of me raring back, getting ready to kick you in the butt). You need to do this!

In the space provided, list out your top ten current debts, and how much you owe on each one.

Here is an example of what this might look like:

1. Mortgage $250,000
2. Car loan #1 $30,000
3. Car loan #2 $25,000
4. Credit cards $10,000
5. Student loans $40,000
Total debt: $355,000

Understand, this is not to discourage you, but you need to see what your actual debt is before you can put together a plan on how to deal with it.

Fill in your current total debt below:

1._____

2._____

3._____

4._____

5._____

6._____

7._____

8._____

9._____

10._____

Total:_____

Manageable Debt vs. Debt Free

In the off-the-grid community, we always talk about finances, such as being debt free and how we support ourselves. I will tell you this from first-hand experience, most of us living this lifestyle are debt free. I don't say this to douse your dream, but to give you a bit of reality. Even if you were not pursuing a life off the grid, I would still emphasize living a debt free life. It is no secret today that we live in a society of ultimate consumerism. Studies have shown that having more stuff doesn't actually make us happier, it just keeps on the revolving wheel of work more so you can spend more.

If you are serious about this lifestyle, you are going to have to seriously analyze your current financial obligations and how you can become as close to debt free as possible or completely debt free. It is pretty straight-forward, if you cannot manage your finances in your current lifestyle, how are you going to do it while living off the grid? The simple answer is: You are not. You need to develop financial discipline before you start implementing the next step of your plan, so that way it is second nature.

Now let's take a look at your monthly expenses, as compared to your monthly income. Here is an example (family of four) of how to comprise a list of monthly expenses:

1. Mortgage/rent $1,000
2. Car loan #1 $500
3. Car loan #2 $350
4. Insurance (all house, renters, auto, medical, etc) $500
5. Student loans $700
6. Groceries/eating out $1,000
7. Clothes $100
8. Utilities $200
9. Credit cards $500
10. Entertainment $500
Monthly expenses total: $5,350

Total monthly income $6,000
Extra monthly income after expenses $650

I think I was generous, as numerous recently studies show most Americans have less than $1,000 in savings and zero saved for retirement ... don't be one of these people! I'm sure you are saying to yourself, "Way to be the poo in the punch bowl, Gary!" I do not do this to discourage you by any means, but

Below list ALL your monthly expenses:

1. _____

2. _____

3. _____

4. _____

5. _____

6. _____

7. _____

8. _____

9. _____

10. _____

11. _____

12. _____

13. _____

14. _____

15. _____

Monthly expenses total:_____

Total monthly income:_____

Extra monthly income after expenses:_____

I know the financial condition of the average American all too well, and this is flat out the elephant in the room. Matter of fact, if you never decide to pursue living off grid, I hope you take the above information and at least pursue a life of financial freedom by becoming debt free. It will make your life far less stressful and give you the ability to pursue the things you want to, instead of being another rat in the race.

Developing Your Strategy to Becoming Debt Free

I don't just throw the "Captain Obvious" information at you, but help you come up with a solution. Now I'm no financial expert, but I'm debt free and have been for a long time, while owning a home off-the-grid on 20 acres, truck, travel trailer, additional land, savings to live for a year without income … you get the point. I don't just say this from an analytical pie in the sky perspective, I live everything I talk about and teach … 100 percent! Not to mention, I have consulted and mentored several people over the years on how to get out of debt and stay debt free.

So where do you start paying off your debt? I always recommend starting on a smaller revolving debt, usually credit cards. Why? First, they tend to have the highest interest rate. Secondly, getting that first bill completely paid off has a huge psychological effect. It helps you gain the confidence to start tackling your debt, and not just rocking in the corner sucking your thumb saying you just can't do it.

If you have multiple credit cards, start with the one with the smallest balance and pay it off first. Yes, even if that means you only make the minimum payment on the others. Once you pay that credit card off, cut it up, call the issuer of the card, and have it canceled. Continue this until all your credit cards are paid off, moving from lowest to highest balance. The only time I recommend you deviate from this is when one of your credit cards has an interest rate far higher than the others. Still, pay the smallest balance off first to get your feet wet and develop some discipline, then move to the high-interest card.

If you have the discipline, keeping one credit card that accumulates cash points is a good idea. I have a credit card that collects cash points and I use this extra money to transfer into a savings account. Here is the catch—I pay that credit card off completely every month before any interest can be accrued, so those cash points are like free money! I know very few people have this type of discipline, but, if you can do it, I highly recommend it.

Next, move to the second smallest revolving debt, for most that will probably be student loans. Now you may say, "But, Gary, my car loan is the second largest one." Yes, but usually the interest rate will be lower on that. Another important point is that items such as cars, boats, RVs, or houses can be sold. I have yet to find a buyer for credit card and student loan debt; if you do, definitely take them up on that offer, and if you think that will really happen, I have a unicorn that poops gold nuggets I want to sell you!

As you can now see, this lifestyle is not only about living simpler, but being more self-reliant and self-sufficient. The more self-reliant and self-sufficient you become, the more extra money you will have, as you will have fewer expenses. The other benefit is you will learn a whole lot of skills you never thought you would.

CHAPTER 4

Operation Downsize and Declutter —No Moving Truck Required

When it comes to the initial pursuit of living off the grid, RV living, or just a simpler life in general, you have to come to the reality that you have way too much stuff! There is no way around it: If you want to truly live this lifestyle, you are going to have to change the way you look at what is truly important to you. Do those fifty pairs of shoes (most still in the original boxes) or three sets of golf clubs in the garage really add happiness to your life? Are they necessary? Were they impulse buys? Did you put them on a credit card and rack up more debt? Hey, I'm not saying that to live off-the-grid you will not need shoes (for some maybe) or you can never play golf again, but you need to seriously shift your priorities in life.

As I explained in Chapter 2 describing my journey, it was painful going through all the unnecessary items I had accumulated over my life, but I also knew I needed to do it. What really sunk in for me was the sheer amount of items I purchased that I had hardly, or never, used. To make matters worse, a great deal of these items were packed, unpacked, and moved around the country. It made me realize the system had sucked me in 100 percent! I was the ultimate consumer, just like they wanted me to be. Being the ultimate consumer is a road to nowhere—the unnecessary items you

purchase never truly make you happy, they only guarantee you will never get out of debt, and you will probably work in that thankless job as close to your last breath as possible.

What you need to realize is, for most of human history, we required very few items to not only survive, but also to thrive. Humans are tribal creatures—meaning for hundreds of thousands of years, we relied upon each other for getting resources for the group, not for just ourselves. Everything was shared, so the accumulation of items is a very new phenomenon to humans.

Economic output for most of our modern existence has been static. To give you an example, here is how this was changed by the industrial revolution (the beginning of consumerism). In 1500, global production for goods and services was around $250 billion (today's dollars); today it is around $60 trillion! Simply put, the things we need to survive and thrive haven't changed much in the last million plus years, but how we consume has greatly changed. I have said this time and time again, we don't have as much of an earning problem as we have a spending problem. Don't get me wrong, the way we spend has been, and is still, greatly manipulated by today's global economic system, but in the end we control ourselves and our actions. Once you realize what the problem is, it is much easier to come up with the solution. The main thing I want you to discover is that by us being hugely influenced by consumerism, not only does

Is it necessary?

How will it improve or make my life easier?

Do I need it right now?

Can I afford it?

Can I live without it?

Will it just sit and take up space?

it make us go into greater debt (as explained in Chapter 3), but it makes us accumulate worthless items that do nothing but clutter up our lives.

Today, every move you make, every step you take, every website or social media site you visit, your personal data is being collected and crunched by numerous algorithms so you can be marketed to 24/7. It is for one reason, and one reason only: to get you to buy something you more than likely don't need to keep the wheels of greed spinning. Here is an alarming fact to punch this point home:

The average child aged two to eleven sees more than twenty-five thousand advertisements a year! Globally, advertising is well over $500 billion year. It is almost impossible for you to escape advertising today. Heck, I record all my TV programs so I can avoid commercials and those slick advertisers now split the screen during a show or sporting event, placing those same ads I was trying to avoid. Yep, we are screwed … well maybe not!

Below, I'm going to give you a step-by-step approach to purchase far more wisely than you have in the past, and to start purging all those unnecessary items weighing you down, thus inhibiting you from fulfilling your dreams.

I go through a checklist every time before I purchase an item:

1. Is it necessary?
2. How will it improve or make my life easier?
3. Do I need it right now?
4. Can I afford it?
5. Can I live without it?
6. Will it just sit and take up space?

Straight forward and simple!

Here is a perfect example—I'm an avid mountain and road bike rider. You want to talk about being told you need every shiny item known to man to participate in these two activities? Today, you can easily spend $5,000 to $10,000 on a mountain or road bike. I have met people who will purchase the new model of a bike they ride every year, losing thousands of dollars on a perfectly good bike that is just as good as the new one. On average I purchase a new mountain bike every five to six years and it is the previous year's model on sale, saving me a ton of money. My current road bike is eleven years old and still works just fine. The only time I replace my bikes are when they are worn out, fixing them up isn't worth it, and/or there are numerous technological advancements on the newer bikes.

Throw in all the accessories that are pitched to you—fancy helmet, gloves, riding jerseys, shorts, shoes, lights, gizmo, gizmo, and more gizmos! I have heard every sales pitch known to man from bike salesmen telling me I need the latest and greatest equipment, which has no bearing on the enjoyment or performance of riding my bikes.

I have seen bike riders' garages packed full of old bikes, new bikes, several helmets, parts still in the packaging, you name the bike item, they have it. This is the classic symptom of ultimate consumerism and cluttering. Next time you are walking through your neighborhood, take a look at the status of people's garages. Most are packed to the rafters with useless accumulated junk and never see a car parked inside.

My riding gear consists of padded biking shorts and the same workout clothing I wear at the gym. Yes, I do have a helmet, gloves, and riding shoes (road bike only; I use my hiking shoes for my mountain bike), all of which I have owned for several years. My twenty-one-year-old Ironman watch and fifteen-year-old CamelBack work just the same as the new ones, so why would I replace them?

The reason I give you the above example is not just to show you how I save money, but how by not purchasing unnecessary or redundant items, you ultimately need much less space!

To get your feet wet, put together your top ten list of items to start with below:

1. _____

2. _____

3. _____

4. _____

5. _____

6. _____

7. _____

8. _____

9. _____

10. _____

Steps for Decluttering

Unless you are a step ahead or your living situation is renting an apartment with no garage, I always tell people to start with your garage for two simple reasons:

1. Most people's garages are ground zero for storing useless crap.
2. It will serve as your staging area for the remainder of your stuff when you progress to the inside of your house.

Here is your decluttering item checklist:
1. Have I used this item in the last year?
2. Does it serve a useful purpose?
3. Does it give me any enjoyment (not by just looking at it)?

If you answer NO to these three questions, it is gone—"well maybe," "sort of," "kinda" are not acceptable. You can only answer yes or no!

Now that you have identified these items, how do you get rid of them?

• Yard sale
• Craigslist.com
• eBay
• Pawn shop
• Donate
• Give them away to people you know
• Put them on the curb with a sign (free)

I have used all of the above with great success over the years. The one that has surprised me the most is setting them on your front curb with a "free" sign. Almost never has an item lasted an entire day without someone taking it.

Here is the kicker, you have 24 hours once

you identify the items to put Operation "Get Rid Of" into action. No procrastination, as that is just another excuse to put it off—get it done … now!

Repeat this until your garage is cleared out. The job is not done until you can park a car, or two, or more, depending on garage size. The amount of cars it was built for is the amount of cars that must fit.

Once you have your garage decluttered, you will now use it as a staging area for decluttering the remainder of your house. "But, Gary, you just told me I have to be able to park my cars in the garage." Yep, that means you better hurry! A really good systematic way is to go through a room a week, then to closets and storage areas on the last weekend of the process.

As I hope you can now see, this is a critical stage that must be done before you get into the nitty-gritty of your plan for finding your property and building your off-the-grid house. Not only is getting rid of stuff cleansing for your mental well-being and allowing you to follow the life you want, but it teaches you the discipline you will need to live this type of lifestyle.

Here is a good piece of advice and something that I do on a regular basis. Just because you go through your initial decluttering process, you are not done. Twice a year I go through a decluttering process: once for my RV, and once for my off-the-grid house. Yep, collecting useless items can sneak up on you if you do not do this. Before you know it, you are right back where you started if you are not careful. The best part of doing this is it doesn't take that long if you consistently do it. For me, it is mainly building supplies and tools that I needed for a certain project, but no longer do. See at right a photograph of my decluttered home office at my off-the-grid property.

My decluttered office.

CHAPTER 5

The How-To Step-By-Step Process for Finding Your Dream Piece Of Land

The next couple chapters in this book are going to be focusing on putting together the pieces for your off-grid project and estimating how much your project is going to cost. The primary reason you need to do this is to figure out how much money you need to put away before you get started. There are two ways to do it:

1. You can save for the entire project before you start.
2. You can save enough to purchase the land and do it in stages.

I have seen it done both ways; there is no right or wrong answer. So how did I do it, you may ask? I chose to purchase my land with cash, save for a year, and then started my project. From there on out, I would build for five to six months, stop, save for the remainder of the year, then repeat until it was done.

Some of you may be asking, "Why don't you just get a construction loan and get it done all at once?" There are two reasons: first, at this time, no conventional financing exists for building off-the-grid houses. Secondly, our goal is to be debt free and not have the burden of a home loan. I have an entire section on this topic in my book, *Going Off The Grid*.

How to Find Your Land

Once you have finished the initial step of life simplification and decluttering, you are ready to get to the good stuff ... starting the research to find your dream property. You will also start the process of determining how much that dream piece of land will cost. Below I will describe the process I used when finding my land, as I believe it will save you a lot of time. For me, even having a background in real estate investing, this was more difficult than I first imagined. Today it is getting harder and harder to find good, affordable land. With that being said, it is still possible, but it takes patience and dedication to your plan.

Since I started my "Off-The-Grid Project," many have asked me how I found my ideal off-grid property. Those who have seen it have even noted that the land and view look amazing, and I'd like to humbly agree.

But as to the question of how I actually found it ... well, that is not an easy question to answer. It didn't happen overnight, and there is no magic formula for finding a great place to get off the grid. As I have discussed previously, my property is unique to my wants and desires, and yours should be specific to your own goals as well. With that being said, I think I have come up with a decent method for locating and evaluating potential properties that will work for most. If you are looking for an easy formula for finding the perfect

off-the-grid spot, I will warn you: There is no easy way. It will take time and a great deal of work. Having said that, I hope my story and strategies will be of some use to you.

Where My Plan Came From

My plan to finally make my dream a reality was originally hatched about ten years ago while I was living in New Mexico during my employment with the federal government. Anyone who has been to New Mexico knows there are numerous outdoor activities in the area in which a sports-inclined person may participate. In that way, New Mexico brought back memories of my childhood growing up in a small town in the Sierra Nevada Mountain Range.

By that point in my career, I had been fortunate enough to have done a great deal of traveling while working in the government. Because of this broad geographic exposure, I already had a few places I was looking at in terms of buying my ideal off-the-grid land.

At the top of my list was Washington State. This was for three reasons:

1. I love the outdoors, and Washington State has tons to offer in this area.

2. Affordability: When I compared land prices in other states, such as Idaho, Montana, and Wyoming, Washington definitely offered the most bang for your buck.

3. Washington has no state income tax. As a business owner this was a big advantage for me.

I had a friend who lived in Northwest Washington, and I used to go visit him once or twice a year. He lived in a fairly congested part of the state. I knew I wanted something more remote, but I just wasn't sure where. As luck would have it, after a transfer for my federal government job back to Southern California, I was assigned to assist on a case in the northeastern part of Washington State.

While working there, I also met a woman, and we dated for a while. So I was able to explore that part of Washington a bit more, and it was love at first sight (with the area—not the woman, unfortunately).

Now, this was some four years after I had my original idea to eventually live off the grid. I had contacted a real estate agent when the idea hit me when I'd lived in New Mexico years earlier. However, my first blush of enthusiasm quickly dampened because land prices were out of my range due to the pre-recession housing boom being in full effect. But I didn't give up. I knew the prices would eventually come back to Earth. And of course, they soon did.

How I Learned That Patience Is the Key

There is one thing I can't emphasize enough when it comes starting your adventure with a more remote lifestyle: Patience, patience, and some more patience. Again, there is no road map for this type of life. Everyone takes their own path and finds what they are looking for via different avenues.

The part of Washington State in which I finally found my own personal paradise is littered with people who had once aspired to a rural and self-sufficient life, but who didn't do their research first, jumped in too quickly, and flamed out. Every time I mentioned I was from Southern California and described what I was trying to do, a local would give me the look like, "Yeah, right, buddy. You will be gone in less than a year, if even that long."

If you have watched too many shows about Alaska on TV, and think that you can pack up the BMW (a rear-wheel-drive car in the mountains, not a good idea!) with the wife and dog, you are better off just getting your triple-shot, fat-free, sugar-free latte, not too hot, not too cold ... well, you get the idea. My advice for those folks is to just stay home and watch the Kardashians. I kid you not, I met more than my fair share of these types of individuals while staying short-term at a local hotel. These people never make it through the first winter, and honestly, they give out-of-state people working toward a better, simpler life a bad name.

So what does the above have to do with you finding your ideal, rural land?

Here's my hard-won advice. As I have previously discussed you have to be dedicated to the idea of changing your lifestyle, and it should be with real intention and thought, and not just on some whim. By hailing from outside the area in which you intend to build, you will have an uphill climb ahead of you just to gain the trust and respect of the locals. Just remember, you are not the first one to come up with this remote-living idea, and many idiots before you have made dealing with the locals in the area much harder.

Formulating Your Plan

If you think you may want to head off the grid for a simpler and more self-sufficient life, I recommend you begin by asking yourself: Why do you want this type of lifestyle?

Do you want it because it looks cool on TV? (I do not recommend this as a valid reason!) Do you just want a simpler life? Do you want a remote vacation house to get away from it all?

Everyone will have their own motivations, but this soul-searching has a concrete point. Moving away from urban areas has to be something you must truly want to do and a lifestyle you really want to adopt.

There are many variations in what "living a more remote lifestyle" looks like in practice. However, the process of finding an ideal piece of land upon which to build your new home will be similar no matter what your preferences. The only thing that will be different is how remote your piece of property will be.

For me, the best way to start was by traveling to various parts of the United States to see what places I liked most. I needed to come up with a short list of potential locations. I have been fortunate and have spent a great deal of time traveling for my job. But for many people, this may not be a possibility. For those who have no idea where to start, I would begin by looking on the Internet for states or areas that have what is on your wish list (climate, land features, state taxes, laws, and so on).

Below, list your top ten locations that you are possibly interested in. Don't worry if you do not have ten locations, but try to come up with at least five

Your Top 10 Possible Locations List

1. _____

2. _____

3. _____

4. _____

5. _____

6. _____

7. _____

8. _____

9. _____

10. _____

Once you have five to ten locations in mind, search the Internet for land for sale in those places to get an idea of the size of the lots that are available, and what the price range for real estate generally is in that area. There are two main websites I like to use for my cursory search: www.realtor.com and www.zillow.com, as most types of properties for sale are listed on these sites. Of course, don't rely exclusively on this type of search. This is just to give you an idea if what you are looking for is affordable and/or available.

After narrowing your locations down, the hard work begins. I would keep the list to five states (or areas) or fewer, if possible. Just like anything in life, you have to experience it firsthand in order to figure out if it is the right thing for you. I planned my vacations in the areas I was interested in, so I could explore the vicinities.

If you have a total of ten locations from your research, narrow it down to your favorite five. The reason I recommend doing this is that going to ten different places to do your research in-person can be a lot of work. Obviously if there are numerous towns in a general area that is different. I'm talking about narrowing it down to five locations, you can narrow it down within those locations as you visit them.

Your Favorite 5 Locations From Your Initial Research

1. _____

2. _____

3. _____

4. _____

5. _____

Now, don't make the mistake I made, which was jumping right in and contacting a real estate agent who happened to be listed on one of the properties I found interesting. Trust me, this type of blind Internet-based fishing expedition for a realtor is a complete waste of time. The best way is to visit the area yourself, then find a local real estate agent who is either from (or at least very familiar with) the area you think fits your needs. Eventually I figured this out. The right way looks like this: I did all my research first, so I knew exactly what I was looking for, and then found a real estate agent local to the area. If you try to use a real estate agent too early in the process, you will end up looking at land they want you to buy instead of the other way around.

I wasted days going to dumpy, unbuildable lots with a real estate agent who was not well versed in the type of property I was looking for. Lesson learned! At this point I realized I needed to do my homework first rather than relying on the real estate agent to do it for me. As you can imagine, this was a really bad idea.

A point of emphasis is needed here: There are very, very few real estate agents in this country who have any experience in remote locations, and even fewer who understand or have any knowledge of living off the grid. To this day, I have yet to met a real estate agent who lives off the grid themselves or has basic off-the-grid living knowledge. When I say this is going to be your journey, I mean that 100 percent. If you think a real estate agent is going find everything you need without your input and research, you are destined to fail.

Keep in mind also that some remote lots are not listed, as they are "for sale by owner" only. The only way you will usually hear about these "sale by owner" lots is in the local newspaper/swap sheet or drive by and see the for sale by owner sign.

How I Adapted and Changed My Plan

After this failure, my new plan was to spend three to four days traversing the area in which I was interested by car. Take my advice: This is the best way to figure out if that region suits your needs, hands down. I put about 1,000 miles on my rental car in three days. But I'll tell you what, I knew exactly where and what I wanted after that.

Once I had narrowed down my search to a specific place, I needed to find a good local real estate agent.

During this time, I had been getting to know the locals in the town in which I was staying. I asked everyone I could about land and if they knew anyone who had property for sale. This approach didn't get me any new leads on lots for sale, but it eventually led me to the right person to get the ball rolling.

Someone told me I should go to the local bank and see if

they had any foreclosed or short sale properties they were selling. Now, this was an excellent idea, so with my newfound enthusiasm, I headed off to the local bank. I ended up speaking with the vice president of the branch, and asked if they had any land for sale. They didn't, but she knew a realtor at one of the local real estate offices who specialized in the type of land I was looking for. One better, he resided in the same area in which I was considering buying.

It was pretty funny. I didn't even have to get in my car to go to the real estate office. I literally walked two blocks from the bank, and I was there. After introducing myself and outlining my master plan, he said he thought he knew of a property that was exactly what I was looking for. Of course, I was a little skeptical because the last real estate agent had said exactly the same thing. But after he brought up the listing on his computer and showed it to me, I was inclined to think that he just might be right. In addition, he found another lot not too far away from the first one that he thought could work as well.

We made a plan to meet early the next morning and head out to take a look. So the next morning, I met up with my new real estate agent, and we went to see a 20-acre secluded lot with a view of a nearby lake (which was one of my absolute requirements for my property). After weaving through an old logging road for about 45 minutes, we emerged onto the property. It was land still owned by the logging company that had worked the area years back. I mention this because early on I had been discouraged from looking at these types of lots, which I now know is a huge mistake.

Turning a Negative Into a Positive

My first real estate agent—way back in New Mexico—wouldn't give me logged lots to look at. His rationale was that such spots had been stripped bare of trees. His opinion was that for someone like me, who wanted to live in the forest, a lack of trees wouldn't make much sense. Now, this may seem to be logical at first glance, but the opposite is actually true. Let me explain.

It is true that some logging lots have been stripped bare, but I have found this is not always the case, especially with smart lumberjacks on the job. The logging company from which I bought my lot has a business model based on reselling land. They selectively cut trees, which keeps the forest in a condition ideal for someone who wants to develop the land or make a homestead. Pretty smart I would say. A savvy logging company can make money off the trees and then make money selling the lots if they do it right. So now you know.

The logging company that had once owned the lot I eventually purchased left me plenty of trees, as it turns out. They cleared most, but not all the good ones. The remaining trees were not profitable for them to cut, but they were great for someone like me, who was looking to build a house in the woods and live on the property. Now, here is the real genius in their plan. A logging company has to build a "landing" at its work sites. The landing is the spot where all the heavy logging equipment is placed and the trees are de-branched, de-barked, and prepared for transport. In the case of the company that had worked what is now my land, they cleverly opted to build the landing in the spot they thought would be the best building site for a future house.

This was great! The buyer (me!) would have far less work to do, and much less dirt to move, in order to make the lot house-ready. By selectively clearing the trees, the property was appealing to a buyer, instead of seeming like a barren scar. Most people who looked at the lot before me couldn't see the potential, because most real estate agents don't have a clue how to develop such a property. Not my local real estate agent! Both of us walked the property and saw all the potential, not to mention how much of the hard work had already been done.

Here is what we could see:

1) The building site was already established in the best location and was flattened and settled. It would take minimal work to finish. (This is especially important when dealing with sloped land, like on a mountainside.)

2) Because the trees had been selectively cleared already, I wouldn't have to remove literally hundreds of trees to make the property buildable. Plus, substantial amounts of work had already been done by the logging company in building roads that granted access to the site.

Tallying up the combination of earth moving and tree removal, I saved probably around $100,000 (which was definitely not in the budget) and weeks, if not months, of extra labor.

Here is another very important point most potential buyers saw as a negative, but it was actually another big positive. The lower portion of my property has transport power lines running through it. Now these weren't the type of power lines I could tap into for electricity, but the industrial-grade kind that transport high voltage electricity to other parts of the state. Most people would look at these and think "no way!" But that would be a big mistake.

First, they were far enough away and below the living area to not be a concern (you can't see them from most of the property). Second, the power company had to maintain the road used to service it, which went through the lower part of my property as an access road. The power company road leads almost all the way to my upper building area ... that complimentary, ongoing road maintenance is a big-time bonus!

One unknown bonus at the time, since a federally regulated power company owned the roads (to be shared as an easement road for property owners), they are considered private roads. Basically, no one besides the power company and the property owner, or other property owners using them to access their property, have the right to use the road for any reason (except emergency services). To bolster my security and deter trespassers, I was able to get two gates with shared locks between the power company and myself installed (at my cost). The short of it is if anyone is trespassing, I can indicate not only are they trespassing on my property, but also private federal land.

Here's a critical point. If you have only lived in a city, you have probably only driven on public roads maintained over the years by local or state governments. You may not even have heard of private roads. But in many rural areas, roads are private, meaning the people living on them must pay for and arrange for their maintenance. Building, and especially paving, a road is expensive ... to say nothing of fixing the inevitable potholes, cracks, and erosion that appear over time. Plus, you would in theory have to share that cost equally with all your neighbors, which can be hard to arrange.

So I was doubly thrilled that by the time I had bought the land and come back to begin building my home, the power company had completely re-done the road, and it did a great job! This left me with only about 200 yards of road that I needed to fix. That saved me probably another $10,000 and years of work because the road was rough but drivable in a truck with four-wheel drive.

The Upside of Being Flexible

I know what you are thinking, "Gary, this all sounds great, but how much did this amazing piece of property cost you?"

Here's the best part. It was a great price because no one had seen through all the supposed negatives. I bought 20 acres of gorgeous mountain land for $23,000 (to include closing costs). No, there is not a misplaced comma—that is twenty-three thousand dollars. That is far less than what most people pay for their yuppie, I'm-really-cool, competing-with-the-Jones' sports car they really can't afford.

As I've said before, a little luck helps in the process, but I wouldn't plan on getting lucky. I had already planned on how to deal with the road issue, but fortunately I didn't have to. That was my lucky break.

You can see that by being patient and doing research, I had made something that seemed impossible for the Average Joe become a reality. I hope my story helps you save some of

the time and effort I wasted and that you find your dream land soon.

Coming Up With Your Land Budget

I know you are probably asking, "Why didn't we cover coming up with your budget at the beginning of this section?" I know it seems counterintuitive, but until you actually do your cursory search, coming up with a budget is a complete waste of time. Until you know what you are looking for and the prices in those areas, you are spinning your wheels. Now that you have some basic pricing and lot sizes in mind, put a budget down below that you are comfortable with. Here is my advice to help you come up with a budget.

1. Determine your minimum acreage size, such as 10 acres.
2. Determine your preferred acreage, such as 20 to 30 acres.
3. Have a preferred range, such as $40,000 to $50,000.
4. Establish a max you are willing to pay; this is different from your preferred range, such as $75,000.

* I can't emphasize this enough, purchase your land with cash. Unlike your off-the-grid house that cannot be financed, your land can, but don't do it! Land loans have much shorter terms and higher interest rates. Buying your land is half the battle. Once you purchase it with cash and own it outright, you can take your time, save, then move on to the next phase of your plan with minimal pressure. Best yet, no debt!

Minimum acceptable acreage size:

Preferred acreage size:

Preferred land budget: $

Max land budget: $

The above is not just for you, but your future real estate agent, if you use one. Real estate agents are not mind readers; the more information you give them, the easier it will be on the both of you. One of my goals is for you to have all this information written down so you can put into a master document at the end for your reference and/or to give to your real estate agent.

I would love to give you what to expect on what is a good price for a piece of land, but there are so many factors involved, such as lot size, location, does it have a creek or other water source, views, etc. It will boil down to what you are comfortable spending and your financial resources, and that is just something I can't do or determine for you.

I will say from my research, while looking at hundreds of lots, it is still possible to find a decent sized lot for under $50,000, and, in some cases, a bit less. The kicker is the cheaper it is, the more challenging it will be. The reason I was able to get such a good deal on my land was that no one wanted to put in the effort to build on it. For me that was perfect. I was looking at building off the grid anyway, so it being raw land (meaning zero access to public utilities, no infrastructure for a dwelling, and unmaintained roads) was no big deal.

CHAPTER 6

Bye-Bye, Greedy Utility Companies—Putting Together Your Off-The-Grid Infrastructure

This is where most off-the-grid budgets get off track, mainly because most forget to add it to their overall budget. We are used to turning on the faucet and getting water, flushing our toilet, turning on our lights without thinking about it. Today, for most, the public utility companies in our town/city take care of all this for us, all we do is pay the bills for the service.

When living off the grid, you are your own utility company, meaning you are going to have to create the above from scratch. Some land will have the infrastructure already done, or at least a water well, but I have found that to be very rare. In most cases, when looking at land to live off the grid, there will be nothing there; you will have to do all the work and get the proper permits. I go over this in great detail in my book *Going Off The Grid*. I want to use this section to give you an idea of the costs of these items, so you can put it into your budget. Trust me. This is important, as I underestimated the cost of my water well by more than $10,000, throwing my budget off for that year.

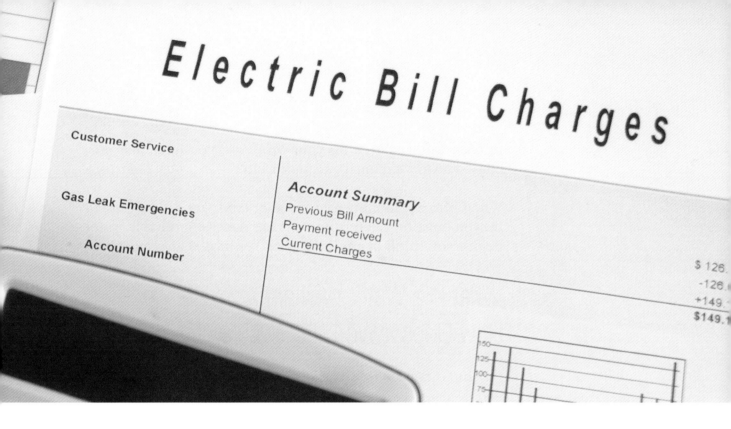

Electric Bill Charges

Customer Service

Gas Leak Emergencies

Account Number

Account Summary
Previous Bill Amount
Payment received
Current Charges

$ 126.
-126.
+149.
$149.1

The Components of Basic Off-the-Grid Infrastructure

To get started, we need to discuss what exactly your off-grid infrastructure is composed of. This tends to be one of the trickiest parts for most people, because it is something they have never dealt with or even thought about. There are three main pieces that will comprise your off-grid infrastructure:

1. Water
2. Septic
3. Power

Water

If you want to live off the grid or in a more remote location, your first and biggest problem will be how to access water. As basic as this seems, you would be surprised how many people ignore this simple, yet necessary, component in the off-the-grid lifestyle. We are so used to turning on the faucet and getting instant water that we forget how precious this resource is and how hard it is to get when not connected to the public utility system. I say this all the time when being interviewed about living off the grid, "If you don't have a reliable water source on your property, you have just purchased a very expensive camping site."

When initially looking at a piece of land you are interested in, you must first determine if it has access to reliable water before you think of anything else. Yes, it is that important.

What Is a Water Well and How Does It Work?

I want to start off with the most common type of system people use to have water on their off-the-grid property: a well. A water well is simply a hole dug or drilled into the ground that provides usable water. We will be focusing on a drilled well conducted by a professional company. Can this be a "do-it-yourself" project? Sure, but for most of us this just isn't realistic. Thus, I will focus on how to hire a professional company to provide your property with a reliable water source. I go into far greater detail discussing various types of sources of water in my book *Going Off The Grid*; this section is primarily for your budget purposes.

Requirements and Expectations for Well Drilling

So what do you need to get water from deep underground? First, a well-drilling company will bring a drilling rig, which is a large truck that uses metal pipe to drill down in the ground until a water source is reached. These tend to be very heavy, large vehicles. They need to be larger if the projected difficulty of finding underground water increases, so having good access roads is vital for your well to be drilled.

A common drilled water well consists of a drilled hole, a casing to line the hole so it does not collapse (usually a sort of pipe about four inches in diameter that reaches down to the bedrock), an electric-powered pump (needed to pump water from within the well to the surface), and a well cap (which stops contaminates from entering the well). Expect to pay from $40 to $50 per foot of drilled well depth for all the previous listed components. This is a general guideline, and will obviously change depending on numerous factors, but I have found this to be a fairly consistent cost estimate for a professionally drilled well.

The well hole is simply a hole drilled into the ground by a drill bit attached to sections of pipe. However, these are not the same kind of wells your great-grandparents may have used back on the farm. Have you ever seen an old-fashioned well with a bucket on a rope attached to a winch? An outdated well like this might be twenty or thirty feet deep, and it would reach water caught in deep layers of mud ... so yes, it was not always very sanitary or pleasant to drink, but it was what was available in simpler times.

In contrast, a machine-dug modern well is very deep, sometimes reaching hundreds of feet below the surface (my well is 510 feet deep). This lets you reach water that has passed through the layers of dirt on the Earth's surface and has filtered down to the hard bedrock beneath. This water is very clean and pure and is exquisite to drink. In fact, once you taste fresh well water you will hardly be able to believe you drank city water for most of your life!

Note that the depth needed to find fresh water in bedrock depends on the geology of your area. In some places in the country, you will need to dig 800 feet or more to hit water reliably; other places require only a hundred or so feet. Well-drilling professionals will typically be able to tell you how deep they usually need to dig in your area to hit bedrock, which is an important number for budgeting since you are charged per foot of drilling.

Also ask about success rate: If you live hundreds of feet above a plentiful underground aquifer, it will be easy to drill for water. However, some areas have water running in cracks in bedrock, which must be blindly targeted from above ground to hit water. Success is not guaranteed. In such cases, if water is not discovered the first time, you may have to pay to drill more than once on your property, and once the entire length of the drill shaft is used.

Indeed, with a modern well, drilling goes as far down as required until an adequate supply of water is reached. Supply is measured in gallons of water per minute (the amount of water measured when pumped from a given well). There is no absolute on what is considered an adequate amount of water by the above standard, this is completely dependent on your needs and expectations, such as how many people will be living in your house.

A workable well usually needs to produce a minimum of one gallon of water per minute. Now, I know you are thinking that is not very much water! How would you even be able to take a shower with that low of an amount of water? We will discuss this idea in a moment. But first, I'd like to share my tips for picking the right people to drill your well.

Choosing a Well-Drilling Company

Considering access to water on your property is going to be key to the success of your off-the-grid lifestyle, choosing a good well-drilling company is very important. In fact, I spent months researching local companies, and getting quotes for drilling my well. This is not a venture you want to mess up, which is why I'd like to share my hard-won advice about the best way to choose well-drilling professionals that will do a good job.

Here's how it played out in my experience. I moved through several states to go off grid, and unfortunately, I found not being from the area made it even more difficult to get a good well team. I decided to use the tried-and-true method of getting three different quotes from local drilling companies. I picked one large company out of a neighboring big city, and then two small, privately owned companies closer to my property.

Just as when I went about hiring general contractors (a topic we will cover in depth in another chapter), I proceeded with great caution. I did not hear anything negative about the two small companies, which was a good sign, but I had to take that with a grain of salt, since contracting companies of all kinds can be notoriously unreliable.

The two smaller companies ended up giving a lower quote than the bigger company, but not by a significant amount.

Even though the larger company had a higher estimate, I decided to hire them to drill my well. Here's why:

- They have been in business for almost 25 years.
- They had the most experience drilling wells in my area and in remote areas.
- They had—by far—the best equipment.
- I knew it was probable that I would need a relatively deep well, and they had a drilling rig large enough to handle digging a very deep well quickly and efficiently.
- I knew the odds of them being in business over the long haul were far higher than the smaller privately owned companies, due to their reach, history, and breadth of established client base. This was important should something go wrong with my well in the future.
- They demonstrated the most knowledge and understanding of my unique project.
- They had no problem with the difficult roads and remote location of my property.
- They were very easy to deal with, and explained the entire process to me in a way that was helpful and proved that they knew what they were talking about.

Fogle Pump (www.foglepump.com) is the larger company I ended up going with. They are exclusive to the Northeast Washington and Northwest Idaho areas, and I'm not sure how far they travel for drilling services. However, I thought I would mention them for anyone who might be looking to drill a well in these areas, since I have had nothing but a positive experience with them. To this day, they have been incredibly responsive to any questions I have had. In addition, they handled all the permitting and water testing requirements for my county, so it was a very painless process.

In the end I was glad I went with Fogle Pump, because my well ended up being 510 feet, which is pretty darn deep. They knocked it out in two days, which is also really good, because they had a powerful drilling rig that could do the job. If I had hired the smaller companies, their smaller rigs would have taken much longer to reach that depth.

As you all know, I'm all for supporting smaller, local companies, but in this case it was better to go with the bigger business that had more experience dealing with my type of property. If my land was not at the top of a mountain, and hadn't require the depth of drilling that it had, I would have had no problem going with a smaller mom-and-pop company. As always, the right choice for you should depend on your unique situation.

Understanding Gallons per Minute and Static Water Level

No matter how professional your well-drilling team is, it's important to know that not all wells deliver the same experience at the faucet.

Some wells have a larger capacity, are more powerful, and refill more quickly than others, creating a faster, more reliable, more powerful flow of water at your kitchen sink. Some are the opposite, and lead to unreliable and weak water flow out of your taps. Because of this, it's important to understand the measures and terms used to describe how effective and powerful a well is, so you can make an educated decision on whether you need supplementary systems to boost the effectiveness of your well-water delivery.

Static Water Level: Once you drill the well, water will typically rise upward—from the absolute bottom of the well to some distance below the surface and then stay there. This is called the static water level, and it is measured as the distance from ground level down to the water in your well. It's the "resting" level of water when you are not pumping and haven't pumped recently. The official static water level is usually measured after twenty-four hours without any pumping activity in your well. The drilling company will provide this number to you in their final report.

For example, my well is 510 feet down to the bottom, and my static level measured at 235 feet. This means that, after twenty-four hours of non-usage, 275 feet of my well shaft is filled with water, which is pretty good. Remember, your static water level is important because this reflects how much water the well shaft can store for you.

However, in terms of production, my well is on the low (dry) end, and produces only three gallons per minute. Even though my gallons per minute is not especially high, my static level is. This means that, overall, it's a good well. Why? The odds of me using 275 feet of resting water in the well shaft in a short time period, on top of my 3 gallons per minute, is highly unlikely. Remember, the well refills itself slowly over time.

What if I wanted an even more productive well? We could have continued to drill, to get better gallons per minute, but in my case, my needs did not require me to do so. Remember, if you are going to live a simpler lifestyle, you are not going to be watering lush lawns nor will you have extravagant landscaping that will take vast amounts of water to maintain. Plus, if you plan to be completely off the grid, don't forget that a well pump needs electricity. In order to get that water to the surface, you will be draining your off-grid power system stores. Very deep wells typically require the most powerful pumps to push the water to the surface, so there exists a very practical trade-off between depth (and cost) and ongoing power requirements that you will have to consider.

There are many solutions when it comes to wells that do not produce enough water for your needs such as storage tanks, but I think this may confuse a lot of people just starting out, and it is usually the exception and not the rule. I do discuss it in *Going Off The Grid* for those who are interested. So now to the cost.

On average today, it costs $40-$50 per drilled foot for a well. This includes the drilling, casing, submersible pump, permits, and water testing. As an example my well is 510 feet deep:

510 X $50 (always use the higher number for budget purposes) = $25,500

As you can see, wells are not cheap today! Drilling my well cost more than my 20 acres of land, but again without it, living a comfortable life on it would be much more difficult.

When initially looking to purchase your land, call around to at least three well drilling companies, and ask about the average cost per drilled foot for a completed well. In addition, give them the location of the property, and ask if they can perform a survey of wells in the area. This will give you the likelihood of finding water on your property and what the average depth of the wells around you. Below put in your numbers to get your estimate:

Average depth of well in your area (   ) X $50

There are three other ways in order to obtain water on your property, and they are creek/river/lake/pond, water catchment system, or transporting water on a regular basis.

Cost of System Where Usable Water Source Already Exists on Your Property

If you find a property with a creek/river/lake/pond, your system will be pretty straight-forward and not very expensive, when compared to a deep well. It will primarily consist of a water pump, water line, filtration system, and a storage tank.

Here is the catch—in the United States there are a mind boggling number of laws when it comes to using water from these sources even when they are on a private piece of land you own. Before you go this route, you need to check with the city and county before you move forward. If you do not do this and break any laws, the fines are steep and financial ruin is very likely.

There are a lot of factors that go into putting together a water pump system, but this should give you an idea for budgeting purposes.

DIY cost, $2,000 to $3,000
Professionally installed, $4,000 to $5,000

The additional costs of a filtration system (not professionally) installed can be up to $5,000 so keep that in mind, as that is not included in the above because of the numerous factors when putting together such a system.

I have seen these systems creep into the $20,000 range, but that is professionally installed with a very large storage tank, high capacity pump, and more complicated filtration/purification system.

Put in amount of type of system you think you will use here: $

Cost of Water Catchment System

Water catchment systems are very popular in off-grid homes in areas that traditionally receive a lot of rainfall, such as Hawaii. Also called rain harvesting, these simple systems connect downspouts (gutters) to a central water tank capable of holding from 500 (low end) to 10,000 (high end) gallons of water.

Again there are numerous factors such as length of gutters used, and size of metal roof (yes, you will need a metal roof to use this system).

On average to do this system correctly, again not including water filtration/purification system, the costs are $500 to $5,000.

Put in your best guess estimate here: $

Transporting Your Own Water

This is simply using a utility trailer with a water safe storage tank to transport water to your property when needed. If you are looking for a fairly comfortable and stress free life, I would not recommend going this route as a permanent solution. But with that being said, getting a reliable water system in place can be pricey, so some will get water this way until they have enough money to put in their system.

For a good trailer that can handle the weight of 250 to 500 gallon water tank, you are looking in the $2,000 to $3,000 range. It can be done cheaper, but I always like to estimate on the higher end.

Where do you get your water to fill your tank? Well, that is the trick; some rural areas have a water pump station that you can pay by the gallon (sometimes free; not very common though) or you will have to figure it out, which is not a fun experience.

Put in the amount you plan to spend on a trailer and water tank, which can be easily found on the internet: $

My Advice For Water System Cost Estimation

Unless you already know you are going to have to drill a very deep well (500 feet or deeper), I would estimate $20,000 for a water system. Sure you can spend less than this, but it gives you some wiggle room. For a deep well, if you are going that route, I would estimate $30,000 to $35,000.

Your water system is going to be the most critical and, very possibly, the most complicated part of your system, at least in the beginning. I will tell you though, I don't regret the $25,000 plus I spent on my well water system for a second. I have reliable pristine water, which not only gives me peace of mind in the drought-ridden state we are in now, but also the health benefits are a big plus. I know exactly what is in my water and where it is coming from, and it doesn't get any better than that.

Estimating the Cost of a Septic System

In this section, I'm going to give the basics of gravity-fed and pressure septic systems. I get asked about self-composting toilets and outhouses all the time, but most people are not going to go this route. I cover the good and bad of these in *Going Off The Grid*.

Standard Gravity-Fed Holding Tank Septic System

The gravity-fed system consists of four components: a pipe that carries waste from the house, a septic tank wherein solid waste contents are stored, a drain field that spreads the waste water out and away from the house, and microbe-containing soil to do final filtering and cleaning of liquid waste.

This is a simple description of the standard septic tank system; it really is a basic system. This is the most common type of system for people not hooked up to public utilities. As a matter of fact, this is the type of system my family and I used during my entire childhood.

For this type of system to be accepted and approved by your city/county, a couple things typically need to be in place.

1. An approved engineer must design and draw the system. This proposal must be submitted to the city/county for approval.

2. Test holes must be dug at the proposed septic site, and the results of these tests must be approved by the city/county. The purpose of the holes is to make sure the below-ground geology is appropriate for drainage; usually these holes must go six feet or deeper without hitting solid rock, so the liquid waste has an adequate drainage area.

3. All the proposed building materials for the system must be approved by the city/county prior to final installation.

So, where should you put the septic drain area (also known as the septic field)? Note that some types of topography make it unlikely that your septic system will be approved. For example, if you are high on a steep slope, or near a main river, local building codes may make it impossible to obtain a permit. Codes may also be somewhat arbitrary, such as how many yards must separate your septic field from that of your closest neighbor.

Another factor to keep in mind is that many building codes

preclude any structures from being built on top of septic fields. This means it's usually imprudent to place your septic field in the exact spot you dream of placing an outbuilding, solar array, or pergola-covered patio. This is yet another factor to check with your city or county before you build.

So where is the best location for your septic system? The best place is usually downhill from your house, so the force of gravity moves waste from toilet to tank, and eventually to the drain field. Thus, this type of system is also called a gravity flow system.

If you cannot use gravity and/or cannot find a deep enough area for the drain field, you will have to use a pressure-based septic system.

I have met more than one person who has done a gravity-fed system DIY, but all of them have had access to heavy machinery. I looked into doing mine myself, and to be honest there just wasn't enough savings to justify the time and energy.

The average cost of a gravity fed septic system is $3,500 (DIY) to $5,000 to $7,500 (professionally installed to include permit).

If you know you can use a gravity fed system, put in the high range estimate here: $

Pressure Distribution Septic System

A pressure distribution septic system is made up of five major components: a dosing tank that collects liquid discharge; a pump that moves the liquid out of the dosing tank and into the drain field; controls for floats, a timer, and to turn the pump on and off; manifolds to distribute the septic liquid discharge to lateral lines; and lateral lines with holes that evenly distribute the liquid into drain field. This type of system will have to go through the same city-/county-approval process as previously outlined for the standard septic tank system.

Compared to a standard gravity-fed septic system, a pressure distribution system is far more complex, but in the end does the same thing. The pressure distribution system does cost much more, but it solves the problem of dirt that is too shallow for a gravity-fed system to work properly.

For cost and ease of use, you ideally want to use a standard gravity-fed system. The only instance in which you will have to use a pressurized system is if your property does not meet the drain-field depth and/or gravity-fed requirements. (Something to consider when buying a piece of land in the first place!)

Here is the snag, even if you have a great gravity-fed system site, an unscrupulous installer may try to talk you into the pressurized system, because they can make more money off you ... a lot more money!

If I hadn't grown up in a rocky, mountainous area similar to my current off-grid Washington property, I would have had no clue that installing a standard gravity system was an option.

Fortunately, I did know, since the first two local septic installers I spoke to tried selling me some song and dance that my property couldn't support a standard gravity-fed system. Again, I was familiar with this type of system and knew better. I finally found a septic installer with some integrity who agreed with me, and the standard system was installed without any problems.

The average cost of a professionally installed pressure fed septic system is $15,000 to $17,500.

If you know your property doesn't have adequate slope/drainage for a gravity fed system, put in the high range pressure system estimate here: $

Estimating the Cost of Your Alternative Energy System

When it comes to living off the grid, there are many challenges. Probably the most critical, after access to water, is the question of how to manufacture your own power (electricity) for your off-the-grid property.

Notes

By definition, "off the grid" means not being tied to any type of public utility. Of course, you could still use an alternative power source while being tied to the grid, but that is not complete off-grid living. That being said, you can still use one or more alternative power sources even if you do not plan to live 100 percent off the grid. Your solution will just be a little bit different in terms of use, and possibly require different equipment.

Conversely, there are reasons to stay connected to the grid. For example, you may have essential medical equipment that relies on a completely consistent energy source, or the financial incentive programs for green energy in your area may make it vastly cheaper to go grid-tied for the next few years. It all depends on your goals, your land, and your budget.

My hope is that this section will answer a lot of questions about the three main alternative energy systems for your off-the-grid project, and will improve your understanding of what may be the best solution for your needs.

I will say this: The most effective and reliable system is one that incorporates all three of the primary alternative power systems, since they tend to be complementary to each other in varying weather conditions (more on this later). The problem in most cases is that this will not be a practical solution for most people (for example, if you don't have access to a stream for a hydropower solution). Usually, two of the three systems can be utilized by most off-gridders, but it depends on your specific property type, and location. (Again, this goes back to the importance of forming your goals and doing research before buying land!)

Please note this section is not intended to be highly technical, or provide you with template systems, but rather to inform you about the most common alternative power sources, how they work, and most importantly for you planning your budget—the cost. There are numerous books that you can purchase with detailed information about setting up systems from A to Z. For me, alternative energy and off- grid specialist Backwoods Solar has been a huge help during my off-the-grid building process, and I highly recommend them when putting together your system. They can and will send you highly detailed quotes for your system with a component-by-component breakdown.

Another good idea is to research the Residential Renewable Energy Tax Credit before you build, as you could potentially save thousands of dollars on your green-energy-system costs. Also check out www.dsireusa.org for a nationwide listing of many other green-energy financial incentives, which vary by state, county, and local utility providers.

Below I will cover the three primary alternative energy systems most used for living off the grid, and general cost. I have left out geothermal, as this is not commonly used and is usually cost prohibitive for most. I do have a section on the advantages and disadvantages in my *Going Off The Grid* book for those who are interested in more information.

* The solar system pricing estimates will include charge controller, battery storage, and inverter. The reason I do this is almost everyone living off-the-grid has a solar system, then add hydro or wind (sometimes both). Once you have your solar system, the additional components of wind and hydropower will use the same charge controller, (or can come with unit at no additional cost) battery storage and inverter. At this point you are just adding periphery components to your solar system … if that makes sense. Because of this the hydropower and wind power pricing will just include additional components added to complete solar system.

Solar Power 101

So what is solar power? Solar power is when the Sun's light or heat is converted into a usable energy source.

Solar power is becoming increasingly popular and more affordable. Just like the technology behind computers, solar technology keeps improving, making it easier and more affordable to live an off-the-grid lifestyle, with many of the amenities we have become used to in the modern world.

The two most common uses of solar energy are the generation of heat and electricity. The use of solar for generating heat is usually in the form of "solar hot water": those black pipes you see on house rooftops that help heat pool water. The more common type of solar energy used today is the harnessing of the Sun's rays into usable electricity, typically via a solar photovoltaic (PV) system. These are the large black-glass panels you see on rooftops or mounted on special frames on the ground.

Before we dive into a few technical points, let me just say that what I will focus on here is true off-grid solar—that is, a stand-alone system that consists of the panel array, batteries, and a back-up generator that exists solely to provide power for you in your private home, when you no longer have sunlight and/or your storage batteries have been exhausted or need to be charged.

Now, for many, the first off-grid solar question will be: Do we get enough sun at our home to take advantage of solar power? Here is a great tool to estimate the amount of possible usable sunlight, wind or even geothermal in your area: www.nrel.gov/gis/maps.html

Using My Solar System as an Example

Here is my simple way to figure out roughly how much available sun power you will be able to generate per day using a solar panel system.

(Solar panels combined maximum watt output) x (average hours of sunlight per day) x (0.5) = daily sun power generated

Note: In this equation, 0.5 is used as an estimate of power loss due to system inefficiencies and conversion factors.

Using my solar system as an example:

My system at this time consists of 6 X 300-watt, 4 X 315-watt solar panels, which gives me a possible maximum watt output per/hour of 3,060 watts. To convert watts to kilowatts, divide watts by 1,000:

3,060 watts = 3.060 (kW)
According to the map at the link above, the average sunlight per day in my region is 4.5 hours.

So my equation will look like this:

3,060 (watts) x 4.5 x 0.5 = 6,885 watts of average power produced per day (or almost 7 kilowatts per day)

I will say this: the above numbers when compared to my actual power generated by my solar system are almost dead on. Obviously this will vary on time of the year, cloud cover, and temperature.

How can you know what your daily power usage will be? The only way to determine this in an off-grid situation is to list every power-using item you have (or intend to have) and add them up (we will do this in the next chapter). Now, this method is not exact, but that is all that you can do for an off-grid situation. It is possible to design a solar array with the capacity to add extra panels at a later date.

Basic Solar System Components

A solar electric system is made up of much more than just a bunch of black panels. Here are the other components you will need to purchase to make a complete system (as taken from the Backwoods Solar website).

SOLAR MODULES (panels) are installed in groups of one to eighteen-plus modules on a solar mount, which in turn attaches to a building, to the roof of an RV, or atop a metal post or racks in the yard. Together this is called a solar array. Each solar module is wired to the other modules in that array by sunlight-tolerant solar interconnect wiring. Several arrays may be wired to a solar combiner box, where they are all connected to heavier underground wires taking the power to the battery and equipment room.

A CHARGE CONTROLLER is a small wall-mounted component, which receives power from solar, wind, or micro-hydro generators, and controls the flow of power to the batteries. To prevent battery damage due to overcharging, the charge control automatically cuts back, stops, or diverts the charge when batteries become full. A charge control may have manual control switches and may have meters or lights to show the status of the charging process.

BATTERIES receive and store DC electrical energy, and can instantly supply large surges of stored electricity as needed to start or run heavy power appliances that the solar panels or hydroelectric generator alone could not power. This large power capability can be a fire hazard just like utility company power, so fuses and circuit breakers on every circuit connected to a battery are essential. Battery size is chosen for both surge power requirements and for the amount of reserve power needed. Typically, 2 to 12 square feet of batteries weighing 150 to 5000 pounds are enclosed in a battery box with a vent pipe to the outside.

AN INVERTER is the major electronic component of a power system. It converts DC power stored in batteries to 120-volt AC or standard household power. Short, heavy cables with a large fuse or circuit breaker carry battery power to the inverter. After conversion to AC, power from the inverter usually connects into the circuit breaker box of the house in place of utility lines. The house breaker box routes power to lights, appliances, and outlets of the house. The inverters Backwoods Solar offers for home power come in ratings from 300 to 8000 watts.

A system like mine that uses components as described above costs about $10,000 to $15,000, depending on the type and number of storage batteries.

Solar Power Limitations

Obviously, the biggest limitation you will face with solar power will be how much sunlight you have in the area you plan to live. If you live in a place such as Arizona or Southern California, there is a good chance you can get by just fine solely using solar power (with the right battery storage capacity).

But those of us in less-sunny areas will need to have more than one alternative power system, combined with good battery storage. This is because, when there is no sunlight (such as at night), you will need to have the ability to utilize stored power from your solar or from the other components of your alternative power system. The same goes for less sunny days of the year.

A good battery bank is also important because the Sun's light is not static, meaning you will not have full solar power utilization all the time. Instead, it will vary per the position of the Sun throughout the day. (A note about batteries: These are currently the most finicky parts of an off-grid solar array, in terms of ongoing maintenance and replacement costs. I recommend carefully researching the pros and cons of different battery choices before making an off-grid solar decision.)

At the time I'm writing this, I have 8 X 6 volt lead acid deep cell batteries that are especially designed for off-the-grid power systems. One thing I didn't know before I installed my off-grid power system, is that most storage batteries are not maintenance free. Like I noted above, they are a finicky beast, and will take the most research and tinkering to figure them out.

The model of battery I currently have costs about $400, and weighs about 120 pounds each. If you abuse your batteries, or don't follow proper maintenance guidelines it will cost you a pretty penny! Probably the most important thing to remember, as far as longevity, no matter what type of battery you get is to try and never discharge or let their charge go below 50 percent. I hope to get as close to ten years out of my batteries before I have to replace them. Storage batteries technology is getting better and better all the time, so I'm guessing when I go to replace them I will have much better and more cost effective options.

Solar system on house

Below are my cost solar system estimates for a small, medium and large off-the-grid house:

Small house (less than 500 square feet) $3,000 to $7,000
Medium house (500–1,000 square feet) $7,000 to $15,000
Large house (1,000–2,000 square feet) $15,000 to $25,000

Put in cost of system above that you think you will need here: $

Obviously there are numerous factors that go into the cost of a complete solar system, but I think this will give you a really good idea what to expect.

Wind Power 101

Generating "wind power" simply means using a wind turbine (propeller) to catch the wind and turn a turbine connected, via a shaft, to an alternator or generator in order to produce electric power. Essentially, the system converts mechanical energy (the movement of the wind) into electrical energy.

For wind power, I suggest using a small wind turbine (six-foot diameter or smaller) to supplement your off-grid alternative power system. Larger turbines can put out a great deal of power today, but the cost and size are not within reach of the average off-gridder. Not to mention big wind turbines can make a lot of noise ruining your remote quiet oasis.

With that said, smaller wind turbines have become incredibly affordable: many come in under $1,000 (not including installation). Once you jump past the six-foot-turbine size, the price moves up very quickly. As an example, you can get a wind turbine in the six-foot diameter range for $1,000 or less; a turbine with a fifteen-foot rotor can start to get in the $10,000 range.

On average, a small wind turbine needs about six to seven miles per hour of wind in order to produce a usable amount of energy. Depending on the speed and consistency of the wind in your area, a small wind turbine can produce enough power daily to run a small energy-efficient electric refrigerator.

The good news is most regions of the United States have sufficient wintertime winds to support most off-grid power needs. To find out how it's usually blowing in your area, use this winter wind guide:

www.primuswindpower.com/solarwind-solution

Basic Wind Power System Components

The great thing about adding wind power to supplement your solar power system is that the components are almost the same. You simply tie your wind turbine into your solar power and battery storage system. The new wind turbines have smart technology, so they're already made to be tied into an existing solar panel system.

Cost of the above single small turbine with stanchion (what your turbine is mounted to): $2,000.

Put in cost of wind turbine(s) system here if you plan to use one: $

Hydro Power 101

For people contemplating living off the grid, or who want to supplement their current utility-tied electrical system, a micro-hydro setup is a great way to go, provided that you have a stream running through your property. The downside: Regulations are changing all the time, so you will have to make sure it is permissible in your city and county to use a micro-hydro system. Two things I can pretty much guarantee: It will require a permit, and it will have to be inspected and approved.

There are two characteristics that determine how much power or energy can be obtained via hydropower: "flow" and "head." Flow is the amount of water that flows past a given point in a given time

Primus 46-inch turbine

period. Head is the water pressure, or how hard the water wants to flow. Higher pressure, water volume, or both will increase your system's ability to produce power. A micro-hydro system essentially consists of a length of pipe that captures flowing water in a downhill stream and then uses it to turn a turbine, thereby generating electricity.

You will need to answer four questions to determine which micro-hydro system is right for you:

- *What is the elevation change (from intake to the turbine) over the length of the pipe?*
- *How many gallons per minute of flow are there (minimum and maximum)?*
- *What is the size, type, and length of pipe (if it is already installed)?*
- *What is the wire distance from hydro plant (lower end of creek) to the home or power-shed?*

Hydro-power system

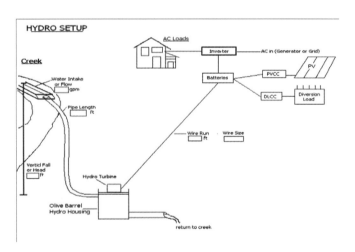

Just as with a wind turbine system, a hydro system can work off the same basic components as a solar array. Now, you don't need to have a solar system to use a hydro or wind turbine system. Just note that the battery storage and DC to AC conversion work off the same components and principles for each system.

That being said, if you do have consistent water flowing through your property, micro-hydro is a great way to go. For that matter, many people use seasonally flowing creeks to supplement their off-grid system—your choice will depend on your resources and needs. Of the three main alternative energy-producing sources, hydro is considered the most reliable and cheapest because water usually runs 24/7, 365 days a year. Therefore, a hydro system is a continuous and cheap power source. This is why hydro is my number one recommendation for off-grid power if you have a way to utilize it on your property.

The cost of a basic micro-hydro power generator and components is $2,000 to $3,000.

Put in cost of micro-hydro power system here: $

In the end, topography, shade, water access, the height of surrounding structures, your budget, local permitting and regulations, and your personal goals in going off grid will all impact your decision of which type or combination of alternative energy systems is right for you.

Propane For Most Off Gridders a Must

Even though you put together a solid off-grid power system, there is a good chance you will need propane to run some appliances such as your cooking stove, clothes dryer, gas heater (required by building code in most cold areas), and water heater (in sunny areas you may be able to use a solar water heating system on your roof). There are two ways to go when you plan to use propane:

1. You purchase larger mobile propane tanks and get the propane yourself
2. You have the local propane company deliver a permanent propane tank (usually in 250-500 gallon tank depending on use) and fill when needed

I would budget $500 (initial cost for tanks and first fill up) for the do-it-yourself route, and $1,000 for propane company setting up and filling tank up for you.

Put in your initial propane tank and filling budget here: $

To Finish Your Alternative Energy System You Need a Backup Generator(s)

This is a really important piece of the alternative energy system puzzle that a lot of people either overthink and spend way too much money, or they don't even think about it at all. I would recommend keeping it simple, especially in the beginning, and purchase at least one off-the-shelf gas generator, but I recommend two. Here is the reason why:

77

To charge your alternative energy system storage batteries efficiently, I would recommend a 7,000-watt or bigger generator, (depending on amount of battery storage you have) and then a smaller multipurpose quiet lighter weight generator, 2,000 to 3,000 watts (uses much less gas than the bigger generator) to use for running tools, moving around property for projects when needed, and is great for people who want to travel in their RV for part of the year.

I personally have two backup generators, the bigger one gets less use now that I have my off-grid energy system dialed in, but my smaller one gets used a lot for projects on the property, and I use it while traveling in my RV.

I would recommend a budget of $1,000 for one, and $2,000 for two generators.

Put in your generator budget here: $

That wraps up the portion for putting together your basic off-the-grid infrastructure. I know for most it seems a little daunting and expensive, but trust me it is worth it to not have to deal with those greedy utility companies! Like I said earlier in this book, when living off the grid, you are your own utility company, so with that comes a bit of a learning curve, but once you get it figured out, it is really not that difficult.

My two generators

CHAPTER 7

The Different Types of Off-The-Grid Construction and What They Cost

In this chapter, I'm going to cover the most common dwelling types most off gridders use. There are so many variables when it comes to building your own home off the grid, but this will give you the basics of construction and what to expect cost wise. For most, this will be the most expensive piece of the project. That is why I save it for last, and why I put the book in the order I think is best to complete your project. Not to mention, when building by codes many counties now require you to put in the infrastructure first. There is a really good reason for this: They know if they let you build the house first, you may not put in proper infrastructure or any at all. Think of people not having proper septic system leaching human waste in nearby streams or worse your neighbor's property ... not a good way to make friends.

Here are a couple other really good reasons to save the house for last. The odds are you are going to change your mind a few times about the type and size of your dwelling. Also don't you think it would be better to develop your building skills on some other small projects, such as shed, garage, and infrastructure before you tackle the house? I do! I have looked at DIY houses on properties I was interested in over the years where the owner was completely clueless, and let

me tell you, the house was not only a death trap, but completely worthless.

Here is a really important factor for being patient building your dwelling at the end. Most of us do not have a deep background in construction, so more than likely, we will need some help with our project. By the time you are ready to build your house, you will have developed solid relationship in your community, thus you will hopefully know some people with a background in construction to assist you.

Most Common Off-Grid Dwellings

The different types of off grid construction listed below are from least expensive to most expensive. Again, there are numerous factors when determining cost, but I will give you an estimated cost per square foot for each type of construction as a do-it-yourself project. To estimate how much it would cost for a professional or house building company to build it for you, multiply your final DIY cost by 2.5. These prices are turnkey prices; meaning this is for a completed house ready to move in with all appliances (not including furniture).

Traditionally framed house

Example:
Say you want to build a 1,000 square foot basic stick construction house (wood 2X4 framing). On average you can DIY for $50 a square foot, so:

1,000 X $50= $50,000 for a completed house done DIY.

For a professional built home multiply this by 2.5:

$50,000 X 2.5 = $125,000

I will warn you that with the shortage of skilled labor and material costs rising, the prices can be all over the place. If you decide to use a professional, make sure to get at least three quotes from referred builders. Remember there is no financing; you are going to have to pay cash, so you need to be very, very careful with the builder you choose if you go this route. I have an entire chapter dedicated to dealing with general contractors in my *Going Off The Grid* book; I highly recommend you read it.

I don't say any of this shooting from the hip. I have been dealing with contractors, building houses, flipping properties, and owning rental properties for more than twenty years, including having a real estate license for eight of those years. Obviously everything I talk about in this book, especially when it comes to costs, are best-guess estimates, but I think I have enough background and experience to get you going in the right direction, and the main goal is to save you a lot of time and money.

The below is not meant to be a detailed guide to how build your house; that is your dream and project and I can't do it for you. There are numerous DIY books and websites where you can find building plans for your dream home. This is to give you basic budgeting and building options so you can then figure out and research your final choice. Also remember building the exact same house in the mountains of Northern California will probably be considerably more than in the mountains in Arkansas.

With that let's take a look at the types of structures you will look at when deciding what works best for you and your property.

Standard Stick Construction

Standard or stick construction is what I consider to be the cheapest in the permanent structure category, and I believe, the easiest type of construction. This is the construction method used to build the majority of the houses in the United States today, primarily because it is cheap, quick, and takes the least amount of skill (my opinion).

Standard construction usually consists of a concrete slab/foundation, but can have a raised crawl space, framed with standard 2x4, 2x6, or 2x8 pieces of wood, depending on your insulation and construction strength needs, and on local building codes. This is the type of construction you will see in almost every neighborhood in the United States. A perfect example of this type of home is the standard tract house.

Average cost per square foot DIY: $50

Yurt

I will make this simple, as that is what a yurt is, so think of a heavy duty round tent. The advantage of using a yurt (I would not recommend it as a permanent structure) is you can put it up very

Yurt

quickly. You will have to check your local building codes—in my county, yurts are considered permanent structures and have the same permit requirements as a permanently constructed house.

Once you deck these out like a normal house, they tend to be cost prohibitive to me, but they are pretty cool.

Average cost per square foot DIY: $60

Earth Berm/Sheltered House

A bermed or earth sheltered house can be built on or partially below grade, with earth covering one or more walls. Sometimes even the roof is covered with dirt and vegetation (think roof garden). The exposed front of the house, usually facing south, allows the sun to light and heat the interior. These types of houses are popular in drier climates with large temperature variances, such as in the Southwest desert.

Matter of fact, I'm in the process of researching building one of these homes in southern Arizona.

Average cost per square foot DIY: $70

Cinder Block/Insulated Concrete Form (ICF)

I will discuss both standard cinder block construction as well as green brick construction, since they have a lot of similarities. The only real differences are what the blocks are made of and the insulation value of each.

Berm House

Cinder blocks are made from a combination of Portland cement and cinders (the dusty remnants of burned coal). In contrast, green brick products are usually made from recycled wood chips and concrete. Green blocks made from recycled wood have a higher insulation value than standard cinder block.

Styrofoam walls filled with concrete have also become very popular but are not really considered green construction. They do have an incredibly high insulation value, however. The downside is that it tends to be a prohibitively expensive type of construction, so I will not be discussing this method.

Block construction is very basic and many industrial and commercial buildings use this type of construction. It simply involves stacking concrete or green blocks into walls and filling open cells with concrete and rebar for strength.

ICF house

The advantages are: a low cost, lower insurance premiums, durability, pest/animal resistance, ease of construction, lower maintenance, good insulation value, outside-to-inside noise reduction, plus they are fireproof.

Average cost per square foot DIY: $75

Log Cabin

Log construction has been popular for a very long time, especially in wooded or mountainous regions. Such areas are usually remote and difficult to reach, so using the surrounding trees as your primary building materials is an easy and practical way to go.

Log construction is simply the practice of stacking notched tree logs in an interlocking pattern. This is how a standard log cabin is built. Log cabins today range from basic to very complicated and ornate.

I know a lot of popular "simple living" type of TV shows have made the log cabin look incredibly simple and cheap to construct, but this is usually not the case. I do know people who have built a log cabin without any outside help, but that is not the norm.

Log House

Conversely, log cabins are usually very expensive to construct when using a general contractor and can be flat out dangerous for the inexperienced "do-it-yourself-er." Think about cutting, moving, and stacking logs that weigh several hundred pounds each. Sounds like a perfect combination of dangerous activities by which you can get yourself seriously injured or killed.

Don't get me wrong, pioneers did this type of construction all the time, but they were a little tougher and more skilled in this area than us modern softies. If you are going to try it anyway, always keep your cell phone handy or have a friend work alongside you. The last thing you want is to be injured during construction, alone in a remote area, without any way of calling for help.

The advantages of traditional log cabins are that they are built from green renewable materials, they are energy efficient and durable, it usually doesn't take much time to construct a cabin, and they look fantastic.

Average cost per square foot DIY: $100 (this will be far less when using and milling your own trees)

Straw/Hay Bale

Straw bale construction is becoming increasingly popular for people living off the grid. These types of houses are usually built in low humidity areas due to possible moisture and rot issues. Straw bale construction employs bales of straw as a structural and insulation material. The straw—which is simply dried stalks of grain—can be from a variety of crops, such as wheat, rice, rye, or oats. Bales can also be made from other fibrous materials, such as bean or corn stalks, pine needles, or any kind of grass.

The easiest way to describe straw bale construction is to think of hay bales stacked on top of each other with construction framing for structural support. The whole thing is then sealed with a stucco type of material. So, if you use straw bale construction, you will still have to frame your house, usually in a manner that is similar to the standard stick construction mentioned above (using traditional framing is usually the only way to meet structural code requirements with a straw bale approach).

The primary advantage of this approach is that straw bale homes have very high insulation values, thus making them very energy efficient. The kicker is this type of construction (when done to proper building code) is much more expensive than people think.

Average cost per square foot DIY: $100

Recreational Vehicle (RV)

Straw bale house

Using a recreational vehicle as a permanent (in most cases, temporary until main structure is done) has been a go-to in off- grid communities since the 1960s. When talking about an RV we are talking about travel trailers, fifth wheels, and motorhomes.

You may be wondering why these are at the end and considered the most expensive? They do have a steeper price per square foot price, but they have more than one function. You have to take the good with the bad.

This is the solution I used, well, I still use, as I spend half the year at my off-the-grid property and the other half in warmer climates during the winter in my travel trailer.

The cost per square foot can vary greatly:

Recreational Vehicle

Average cost per square foot: $50 (older model used) $500 (think rock star touring motorhome).

On average you can get a decent starter RV used for about $10,000 to $30,000

*For detailed information on RVs see my book *The Simple Life Guide To RV Living*.

Tiny House

I know this one is going to throw people off because all those popular tiny living shows make the tiny house seem like some cheap and easy way to live. In reality, whether a DIY tiny home on wheels (think small house like travel trailer) or a permanent structure home (considered 500 square foot or less), they are not as cheap as those shows make them out to be. I would not want to discourage you from a tiny house, well, only if you do not do it yourself, as the construction industry will mark these up to 10 times what it would cost you to do it yourself. I would highly recommend you do not have the rolling or permanent version built by a professional because of the outrageous markup, plus it's a great way to build your skills before tackling the main house.

Average cost per square foot DIY: $50 (standard stick construction) $100 to $150 per square foot for fully livable (mobile tiny house on wheels).

Put your best guess square footage you will require for your off-grid dwelling:

Put the type of construction you choose above with per square foot cost:

Multiply square footage by per square foot cost here to get total estimate: $

If you are going to go the RV route, put in your estimated cost here or 0 if you plan to use one you already own: $

Tiny House

Boy, was that some fun or what! I know it seems a little overwhelming at this point, but by going through this process, you are going to make you life a lot easier. You now have the majority of your plan documented and ready for execution.

If you are possibly suffering from a little sticker shock, here is the good news, the numbers I'm having you use are on the high end of the spectrum. I do this for three reasons:

1. It always cost more than you think it will
2. If your budget is pretty close, your likelihood of success in this lifestyle is much higher
3. It is always better to live in reality than lala land

CHAPTER 8

Creating A List Of Things You Can't Live Without

Now that we have a decent idea of what our project will cost, let's take a look at the things you can't live without, as this will further refine your budget.

An example: Let's say you just can't live without the creature comforts of central heating and cooling like a standard on-the-grid house. This is going to cost you somewhere in the neighborhood of $20,000 to $50,000, depending on the size of house and additional alternative energy components you will need to power this type of system. I think you can now see why almost all off-the-grid homes are very energy efficient and lack central heating and cooling.

Below is the list of the ten things I couldn't live without, which I put together before starting my project:

1. Satellite TV (I know, I know, I'm sports guy though had to have it.)
2. Reliable internet to run my business
3. Cellular reception, again for business
4. Washer and dryer
5. Wood burning stove
6. Standard gas cooking stove

7. Two fully functional bathrooms
8. Enough power to run portable air conditioner
9. Standard electric refrigerator/freezer
10. Standard septic (no composting toilets)

Below, put together your top ten list of things you can't live without. This will help you further determine infrastructure, building requirements, and overall budget of your project. Most importantly, the list will help determine if a property you are interested in will fulfill your requirements.

1. _____

2. _____

3. _____

4. _____

5. _____

6. _____

7. _____

8. _____

9. _____

10. _____

CHAPTER 9

Fine Tuning Your Energy Usage Requirements

The reason I'm putting this section close to the end is I didn't want to overwhelm you in the beginning, and now you have had a little more time to consider what you will be using in the area of appliances and other items requiring electricity.

This is the best way to really see what your estimated daily energy use will be day to day, and what size alternative energy system you will need (a great list to give the company you plan to purchase your components from).

See a brief example below:

Item	Wattage Rating	Run Time Per Day	Watts Used Per Day
Washer/Dryer	2000	20 min (⅓ hour)	660
LED lighting	84 (total)	3 hours	252
TV	80	2 hours	160

Now compute item daily usage:

Item watts X run time per hour = watts used

2000 watts X ⅓ hour per day = 660 watts used per day

You continue to do this for every item using electricity that you plan to use, down to a toaster or curling iron. This is the most accurate way to determine you system. I did this and all I had to do was add a couple solar panels down the road. If you underestimate, doing a system rebuild can be costly.

Alternative Energy System Usage
For Proper Sizing Worksheet

Item	Wattage Rating	Run Time Per Day	Watts Used Per Day

Off Grid Project Total

Record your total debt (Chapter 3):

1.
2.
3.
4.
5.
6.
7.
8.
9.
10.

Total: $

Record total monthly expenses (Chapter 3):

1.
2.
3.
4.
5.
6.
7.
8.
9.
10.

Monthly expenses total: $

Total monthly income: $

Extra monthly income after expenses $

Cost Estimate Worksheets

New purchase checklist (Chapter 4):

1. Is it necessary?
2. How will it improve or make my life easier?
3. Do I need it right now?
4. Can I afford it?
5. Can I live without it?
6. Will it just sit and take up space?

Decluttering item checklist (Chapter 4):

1. Have I used this item in the last year?
2. Does it serve a useful purpose?
3. Does it give me any enjoyment (not by just looking at it)?

If you answer NO to these three questions it is gone—"well maybe," "sort of," "kinda" are not acceptable. You can only answer yes or no!

Top ten decluttering list of items (Chapter 4):

1.
2.
3.
4.
5.
6.
7.
8.
9.
10.

List your top ten locations that you are interested in. Don't worry if you do not have ten locations, but try to come up with at least five (Chapter 5):

1.
2.
3.
4.
5.
6.
7.
8.
9.
10.

List your favorite five locations from your initial research (Chapter 5):

1.
2.
3.
4.
5.

List your land size and budget criteria (Chapter 5):

Minimum acceptable acreage size:

Preferred acreage size:

Preferred land budget: $

Max land budget: $

After getting at least three quotes for your water well, find out the average depth of wells in your surrounding area to estimate your well cost (Chapter 6):

Average depth of wells in your area (   ) X $50 =

If you are going to use a natural above ground water source, record budget for pump and components (Chapter 6):

$

If you are going to use a water catchment system, put in your estimated budget (Chapter 6):

$

If you plan to haul your own potable water to your property, put in estimated budget for trailer and water tank (Chapter 6):

$

Write down your estimated budget for your gravity-fed or pressure distribution septic system (Chapter 6):

$

Alternative energy system estimated budget (Chapter 6):

Solar $
Wind $
Hydro $

Propane storage tanks estimated budget (Chapter 6):

$

Backup generator estimated budget (Chapter 6):

$

Enter the estimated square footage of your house and multiply it by the cost of the type of construction you plan to use to get your construction estimated budget (Chapter 7):

Square footage x type of construction =

If you plan to use a professional home builder for your entire project, multiply the above by 2.5 (Chapter 7):

$

If you plan to temporarily or permanently live in an RV, put in estimated cost (Chapter 7):

$

Now add together all your estimates to get your estimated project budget total (Chapter 7):

Grand Total: $

List your top ten creature comforts you can't live without
(Chapter 8):

1.

2.

3.

4.

5.

6.

7.

8.

9.

10.

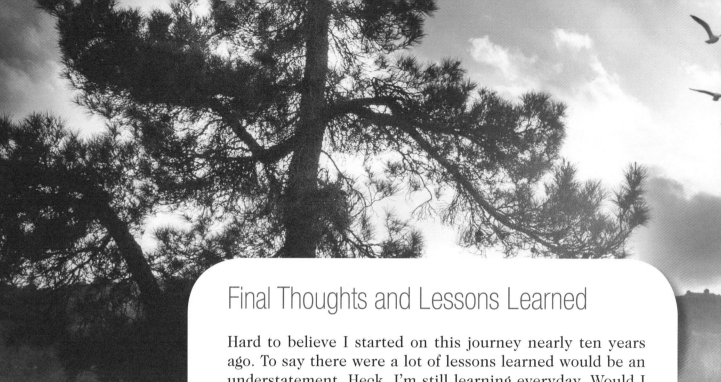

Final Thoughts and Lessons Learned

Hard to believe I started on this journey nearly ten years ago. To say there were a lot of lessons learned would be an understatement. Heck, I'm still learning everyday. Would I change things if I could? Sure, but that is not reality. The best advice I can give is to take it day by day, and don't get ahead of yourself. Also be flexible, as things will change, hopefully not too drastically, but they will change, I can guarantee that.

Budgeting is key. There are too many shows out there today saying you can do it in eight weeks for some ridiculously low amount. Remember that is TV, not reality. On average from the numerous people I have spoken to, including my project, it takes three to five years to complete your off-the-grid house. As with anything today, it costs money, and when discussing the off-the-grid lifestyle in the beginning you need cold hard cash. I'm pretty confident Home Depot or my local lumberyard isn't going to take my used truck tires or bitcoin for payment.

I hope this workbook helps you devise a plan and put it into action. Even if you are not ready right now, I think filling everything out in this workbook to give you an idea of what to expect is worth it in the end. I still have pages and pages of notes and estimates I put together for my project years ago. If it wasn't for an unethical contractor in the beginning of my project, my final numbers would have been pretty close to my estimates.

When I look back, it is hard to believe that my *Going Off The Grid* book on my project caused such a stir, as it was a book I really hadn't planned to write. I was just going about my business trying to live as simple a life as possible, I just

didn't see people being interested in it. I'm incredibly thankful for all the people I have met along the way, and I hope I helped motivate them to pursue their off-the-grid dream as well.

I wish you luck on your project and new lifestyle, I know I don't regret my journey for a second, and I'm pretty sure you will not either!

Did You Enjoy This Book?

You can make a big difference and spread the word! You're a committed group and a loyal bunch of fans!

I truly love my fans and the passion they have for my writing and products. Simply put, your reviews help bring more fans to my books and attention to what I'm trying to teach.

If you liked this book, or any of my others for that matter, I would be very grateful if you would spend a couple of minutes and leave a review. Doesn't have to be long, just something conveying your thoughts. If you would go to www.amazon.com and leave a review it would be greatly appreciated.

Thank you!
Gary Collins

About Gary

Gary Collins has a very interesting and unique background that includes military intelligence, special agent for the U.S. State Department Diplomatic Security Service, U.S. Department of Health and Human Services, and U.S. Food and Drug Administration. Collins' background and expert knowledge brings a much-needed perspective to today's areas of simple living, health, nutrition, entrepreneurship, self-help, and being more self-reliant. He holds an associate's degree in Exercise Science, a bachelor's of science degree in Criminal Justice, and a master's of science degree in Forensic Science.

Gary was raised in the High Desert at the basin of the Sierra Nevada mountain range in a rural part of California. He now lives off-the-grid part of the year in a remote area of Northeast Washington State, and the other part of year exploring in his travel trailer with his trusty black lab Barney.

He enjoyed and considers himself lucky to have grown up in a very small town experiencing fishing, hunting, and anything outdoors from a very young age. He has been involved in organized sports, nutrition, and fitness for almost four decades. He is also an active follower and teacher of what he calls "life simplification." He often says: "Today we're bombarded by too much stress, not enough time for personal fulfillment, and failing to take care of our health … there has to be a better way!"

In addition to being a best-selling author, he has taught at the university/college level, consulted and trained college level athletes, and been interviewed for his expertise on various subjects by CBS Sports, Coast to Coast AM, The RT Network, and FOX News to name a few.

His website, www.thesimplelifenow.com, and *The Simple Life* book series (his total lifestyle reboot), blows the lid off conventional life and wellness expectations and is considered essential for every person seeking a simpler and happier life.

Sources

Backwoods Solar, *40th Anniversary Edition Planning Guide & Catalog*. 2018.

D.J. Holt, P.M. Ippolito, D.M. Desrochers, and C.R. Kelley, *Children's Exposure to TV Advertising in 1977 and 2004*.

Michael Sebastien, "Marketers to Boost Global Ad Spending This Year to $540 Billion," *Advertising Age*, March 24, 2015, accessed 14 October 2018, http://adage.com/article/media/marketers-boost-global-ad-spending-540-billion/297737

Angus Maddison, *World Economy*, vol 1, 261, 264; "Gross National Income Per Capita 2009, Atlas Method and PPP," World Bank Group, accessed 14 October 2018, http://siteresources.worldbank.org/DATASTATISTICS/Resources/GNIPC.pdf

Additional Notes - - - - - - - - - - - - -

Additional Notes — — — — — — — — — —

PLANNING

Additional Notes

Additional Notes

Additional Notes

Additional Notes

Additional Notes – – – – – – – – – – – – – – –